# SEL

# A

# BLUE COLLAR

# VOCATION

# SELECTING
# A
# BLUE COLLAR
# VOCATION

## GEORGE SILBERZAHN

TATE PUBLISHING
AND ENTERPRISES, LLC

This book is designed to provide accurate and authoritative information with regard to the subject matter covered. This information is given with the understanding that neither the author nor Tate Publishing, LLC is engaged in rendering legal, professional advice. Since the details of your situation are fact dependent, you should additionally seek the services of a competent professional.

The opinions expressed by the author are not necessarily those of Tate Publishing, LLC.

Published by Tate Publishing & Enterprises, LLC
127 E. Trade Center Terrace | Mustang, Oklahoma 73064 USA
1.888.361.9473 | www.tatepublishing.com

Tate Publishing is committed to excellence in the publishing industry. The company reflects the philosophy established by the founders, based on Psalm 68:11,
*"The Lord gave the word and great was the company of those who published it."*

Published in the United States of America

ISBN: 978-1-68207-200-4
1. Biography & Autobiography / General
2. Self-Help / Personal Growth / General
15.10.30

# CONTENTS

### The 1940s

### The 1950s

### The 1960s

## The 1970s

## The 1980s

## The 1990s

## The 2000s

## The 2010s

# The 1940s

# OSMOSIS AND ON-THE-JOB TRAINING

What do you want to be when you grow up? I imagine everyone has been asked that question, and very few have had an answer. If a person doesn't have guidance, then circumstance, situation, experiences, and necessity will make the selection. I don't remember being asked that question.

This work is about my experiences as I looked for a way to make a living while not having a specific occupation, or even a general field of endeavor, in mind. It covers seven decades.

I was born without a collar color, the son of a man who worked as a foreman in a DuPont plant he referred to as the Mill. The Mill was what the workers called the place, and management referred to it as the Plant. The "Plant" manufactured explosives and corrosives and other nasties.

The plant was originally a collection of manufacturing units called mills, since what they did was mill black powder into fine, ground gunpowder. Over time, other "explosives" were added to the mix of products.

The Plant was located along the Delaware River, which provided access to good transportation in an area surrounded by woods and swamps and ditches, which was ideal for the manufacture of nasties such as dynamite, nitroglycerin, black powder, and PETN since the manufacture, transport, or storage apparatus for these products tended, on occasion, to explode.

Other nasties were added to the product line manufactured at the Plant. These different operations, as they were called by management, included sulfuric acid, hydrochloric acid, hydrogen peroxide, aniline, and ammonium nitrate, all of which would burn skin and absorb oxygen. They tended to be discharged into the air and water in small amounts. Ammonium nitrate was considered benign, not an explosive. That changed later when Texas City, Texas, was nearly obliterated when a ship full of the stuff blew up.

The surrounding ecology was used to break the concussion that came from one of those occasional explosions, and to dilute discharges that would do bodily and ecological harm.

Workers would report to the plant hospital with pounding headaches (from nitroglycerin) or blue fingernails (from aniline absorbing oxygen) or burns (from acids or from hot steam pipes or steam) or nausea. All accepted as just part of the daily work routine. There was no such thing as the Occupational Safety and Health Administration (OSHA).

One childhood recollection I have is finding myself on the floor of my bedroom, having been blown out of bed in the middle of a warm night. The voices of women in their bed clothes reached my second-floor window as they gathered under the pine trees between our house and the railroad tracks. The railroad transported material to and from the Plant. Their attention was on the skyline beyond the railroad tracks, the baseball and football fields, and the front office building. The sky above the trees beyond the front office building was rose colored; sounds of sirens were coming from there. There'd been an explosion.

I heard the women asking, "Which operation was it? Was Herb working tonight? What about Charlie? Anybody hear anything yet?" All ears, including mine, were tuned to the volunteer firehouse in town. If that bell sounded, it meant there was a call from the Plant for the ambulance—someone was hurt. If there was no call, it didn't mean all was well. There wouldn't be a call for an ambulance if emergency medical service would be of no use.

The Plant spread for two miles along the east bank of the Delaware River and nearly a mile inland to the town of Gibbstown. The town of less than 2,500 people was wedged between the plant and a mixture of farm/orchard landscape in Southern New Jersey.

The town had two sections where houses were built by duPont to rent to employees: the "old village" and the "new

11

village." People there were mostly DuPont employees, but some were not.

There were four other sections: Little Italy (mostly Italian descent), Greens (mixed neighborhood), Crow Hill (unofficial name, mostly black people), and an area without a name (another mixed neighborhood). Mixed did not mean white and black. It was way too early for enlightenment to have brought that about. It was strongly segregated, and the segregation of white people was by class.

The town as a whole was inhabited by mostly blue-collar people. Do farm people have a collar color? There were a lot of farm collared folks. My world was comprised of neighborhood boys. Girls, black kids, and others not like us were there, but just not consequential.

I grew up in Gibbstown, New Jersey and learned about vocations mostly through osmosis and on-the-job training. Parental guidance consisted of "Get good grades so you can get a good job." The twelve to sixteen years which begin at age five were consumed by grammar school, high school, and mandatory military service. Not many went to college or received deliberate vocational guidance. Getting a job meant take whatever you could get and be happy you got it.

We rented a house from DuPont in the old village, where wage roll people lived. The bosses lived in the newer "new" village. The club had tennis courts and was built to provide activities for the families of people who worked in the plant. The official name of the plant was the Repauno Works.

We lived with the back of our house facing Repauno Avenue a block away. Repauno Avenue crossed the railroad tracks on its way into the Mill. There was a one-story building with a rusted tin roof overhanging the front of it that stood facing our house at the crossing of the railroad and Repauno Avenue. There were three businesses in that building. The business next to the railroad was Billy Burt's, a bar; Bouchter's store, where we bought lunch meat, next to Billy's; and an auto repair shop next to that.

We didn't buy milk from Bouchter's. That was delivered to our house by a horse-drawn wagon from Ashton's Dairy, which was on the bend of Broad Street above Greens. In cold weather, columns of frozen milk would be sticking out of the tops of the bottles with the caps sitting on top. Some people still had an icebox, but we had an electric refrigerator, so we didn't need ice delivered. We kids would grab a piece of ice off the floor of the delivery wagons as a treat to eat. I have memories of snatches of times of elevated excitement in the Old Village even though I had little or no understanding of what caused the excitement. Things changed around Christmastime the year I turned three. Everyone became angry at someone called Jap and someone else called Hitler.

# WAR TIME

Most of my formative years were spent in a society in turmoil, but I didn't know that. It was what it was, and I didn't know any different. It was wartime, and there were things a lot of people were doing for the "war effort." We had a Victory Garden where we grew peppers, tomatoes, and other things like that. The whole neighborhood did it. We didn't make sauerkraut because that was German; we made victory cabbage. We also ate a lot of dried beef gravy and corn fritters.

> *It's less expensive to grow or make for yourself what you need.*

During my preschool years, I came to understand that you couldn't buy as much of some things as you wanted due to something called rationing. We had little books of stamps called ration books, and we used them, along with money, to buy things. The year I turned five, I began the task of running down to Bouchter's store at night to get lunch meat and bread for the sandwiches my mom made for my dad to eat for lunch. I didn't need money because we "put it on the book." Mom sent me to Bouchter's with ration stamps when I had to buy sugar. We bought things like boiled ham lunch meat and gasoline in small amounts: 1/4 quarter pound of lunch meat, $1 worth of gasoline.

We had war savings stamp books. We would buy a 10¢ savings stamp every so often, and I got to stick it on a page in the book. When we had enough books filled, we could buy a war bond. I got to give the books to the person at the post office. Later on, I learned the bond would be worth more money than we paid for it if we kept it long enough.

Dad became something called an air raid warden. When there was a 'blackout' drill, he would run around the house putting all the lights out, then put on his helmet, grab his flashlight, and go around the neighborhood telling people to turn off their lights. The cars had the top half of their headlights covered with black electrical tape.

My mom went to work at the plant for a while, as did quite a few of the neighborhood women. In the afternoon, I was taken to the "A Line" gate to meet the olive drab–colored bus that dropped her off at the end of her shift. We walked home together with some of the other women. The A Line was on the left side of the Plant where a branch of the railroad tracks entered. The C Line was on the right side where Repauno Avenue entered, but no railroad tracks. She worked in the shell house packing shells. I think that meant ammunition shells, but that job didn't last all that long, because she was one of those people who suffered severe headaches, so she had to quit.

Uncle Jack, my mother's brother, visited our house for a short time. I saw him in his uniform before he went away to that place called war. There was constant talk about war, which I didn't understand all that much, just that there was something going on that a lot of men were involved in and it was a really bad thing. There were little banners hanging in the windows of some houses. They were blue with gold fringes on them and a white star in the middle. That signified there was someone from that house in the war. If the star was Gold, it meant a person had been killed.

That fall, I turned five and started first grade. Mom would walk me to and from school. The windows had thick screens over them to keep glass from flying into the room when there was an explosion. The year I turned six, I started walking to school myself.

It was around summer when I heard the women talking really excitedly about some special day. They called it a D-day. That didn't mean anything to me but which wave of troops someone was in on that day was really important to them. I thought it was about a trip to the beach.

Winter came and went.

The next year, when Christmas was getting close, the women still gathered at their backyard fences and talked about things while they hung clothes to dry. I was looking forward to Christmas, but Mom and the others were talking about a bulge of some kind in the war. They were very worried about that bulge for a few weeks. I learned the bulge was in the line where the armies met and our army had gotten backed up a lot and was losing.

After that winter, on another sunny day, the women's excitement at the fence was a lot different: it was happy. Church bells were ringing, and sirens were blaring, and car horns were beeping. I stood in our backyard looking around for what was causing all the hubbub. This day was like the Fourth of July because everyone was happy and jumping around. This time it was about something called Victory in Europe Day.

It seemed like just a few weeks later when the racket started up again. This time it was over some day called VJ and some bomb they called atom. That was Victory in Japan Day. The war was over.

# The 1950s

# POST WAR YEARS

After the war, I spent a lot of time in the marshes and woods that were on the other side of the railroad tracks and down a short distance from our house. That was my playground.

I was awakened one morning by clanging coming from the railroad tracks. I went outside to watch groups of men working on the tracks. One group was pulling spikes out of the ties with long, thick crowbars and setting the track aside with what looked like big ice tongs. Another group replaced the ties and then put the tracks back. Plates with holes in them were laid on the ties, and the men would lay a track in place on the plates. A group of four men stood in a circle around a plate—one tapped a thick spike through a hole in the plate, stood up, and swung his sledgehammer over his head to bang on the spike. The man next to him would begin swinging his hammer before the first one was done, and the man next to him did the same, and so on. That was the clanging that woke me up. The rhythmic *clang, clang, clang, clang, clang, clang, clang, clang* was like music as the spike was driven into the tie to hold the track in place.

My trek to grammar school took me about three-quarters of a mile along Railroad Avenue, which was between my house and the railroad tracks. The street would have gone through where Billy's was, if the building wasn't there. I crossed Repauno Avenue going to and from school.

Most days, Jonas Reign's wagon would be parked by the back door of Billy's. That wagon had twisted rail sides leaning inward and outward, wobbly and threatening to fall off at any moment, wheels each leaning a different angle, a seat leaning to one side sat at the top and front, and a swaybacked horse whose head hung as low as its swaybacked belly, stood stark still at the front. When it was moving, all the parts waggled and wavered.

Jonas bought beer by the gallon for $1; he brought the jug. The sight of Jonas in his baggy coveralls slumped on his sloping wagon seat with his gallon jug in the crook of his arm, the horse moving just a touch faster than not at all, wheels wobbling and rails rocking back and forth as he slowly made his rounds picking trash for whatever he might be able to use or sell, was part of the daily scene.

I learned recycling and to repurpose from Jonas long before that was even a glimmer in anyone's eye. Billy sold cigars for 5 cents, and Jonas would allow for a couple of those on occasion. He'd smoke those down to where his yellowing, drooping mustache was singed, and then the stubs of the cigars were cleaned of burned residue and kept in an old cigar box on the seat next to him. When the mood would strike, Jonas would chew the cigar stubs. He'd put his "chaw" out to dry on the roof of the shed where his horse was housed at his home. The township later condemned and burned that homestead to the ground. When the chaws were dried enough, he cut them up and smoked them in a corn cob pipe he had hanging from his mouth.

Coming home from school, I would take a shortcut through Billy's. In the back door, past the dartboard and restrooms, potbellied stove, card tables, pool table, bar with spittoons on each end of the brass foot rail, and out the front door. The place smelled of pretzels and beer taps.

Sometimes a red haired woman who seemed to be there all the time would sit me on a bar stool and buy me a coke. Her name was "Cokey," and some people called her a floozy. She had a horse, named Alcatraz; and sometimes he'd be out back with Jonah's wagon. Her husband, or something, Harvey, was the skinny daytime bartender. He had weak, watery blue eyes and wore suspenders to hold up his baggy pants. His hands shook a lot. There was something wrong with him, but I didn't know what. Cokey let me learn to ride Alcatraz, and I'd ride him around the neighborhood sometimes. I was riding down the street toward Billy's when Denny Meyers pulled up alongside on his 20-inch bicycle: he delivered newspapers. We raced a short distance, and Denny beat Alcatraz. My sister tried to ride Alcatraz, but that didn't work out so well. We never asked for a pony for Christmas.

Billy's was where I learned about the muskrat hide business. The guys who bought hides would stop at Billy's and buy hides from local trappers. They would have contests to see who could skin a rat the fastest. The object was to peel the skin off without tearing the hide, which would reduce the value. The really good guys could get the whiskers and eyelids.

I was given an old "steely" jump trap by someone, and I went off to catch a rat. They were called jump traps because when the trigger pad was released and it sprung closed, it would literally jump in the air. Learning how to catch rats might have been my first vocational education: you can be told something, but knowing how to get done what you're told is the secret.

My next lesson in vocation was in finance. A new steely cost $2.50, and a good brown-haired rat hide brought in $5.00 but a black one up to $10.00. As I bought more traps and my "line" got longer, I learned more about vocations.

> You have to find your line and traps. *You have to invest in your business.*

I'd be in the Frog Ditch marsh just at daylight, and again just at last light. It wasn't long before I had a line of traps and learned some more about vocations. I was on the school bus on the way to high school and saw a guy in hip boots heading for the Frog Ditch.

> *You have to keep the location of your line and sets secret.*

*You have to know how to convince people that it wasn't in their best interest to take your rats.*

Where Gibbstown stopped and the next town, Paulsboro, started, there was a racetrack. Sulky racing, not sit-on-the-horse-flat-track horse racing but ride-a-cart-behind-the-horse kind of racing. I'd thumb it (that's hitchhike) up and watch the drivers working out the horses. I got a job walking horses after their workout, which involved at least an hour of leading the horse in a circle while it cooled down. The job paid $1.

One day there was a show of some kind, and they were short of riders, so they asked us walkers if we wanted to ride a horse in the show. These were not the sulky horses; they were show kinds of horses. I had experience riding Alcatraz, and they said they'd show us what to do and it would pay $1, so I volunteered. I did fine at the walk and the trot and the gallop, but the canter got me. Alcatraz didn't do canter. I couldn't time me and the horse's ups and downs, and so I was coming down when the horse was going up. My life as a show horse rider was over before it began.

As a walker, after the cool-down walk, I would take the horse back to its stall in the barn, and the groom would wash it down and put it in the stall. I had a stallion to walk the last day I had the job. This day was really hot, and I wanted to get in the cool shade of the barn as soon as I could. The stallion's stall was on the end of the barn, the far end. So instead of walking all the way around the barn in the sun, I took the cooler path, through the barn. That was why it was my last day on that job. Who knew that walking a stallion past stalls of mares would cause such an uproar? First thing I knew, I was dangling from the bridle as the stallion was rearing up, whinnying and swinging his hooves.

In the woods, across the tracks and a little down from our house, there was big patch of huckleberry bushes, if you knew where to find it. I did, and so did some of the ladies from the old village with their straw hats and mosquito netting hanging from the hat brims all around their heads. If you could put up with the horse flies, mosquitoes, and blazing sun, you could pick a bucket of huckleberries in a couple of hours or so. A bucket of huckleberries could be sold in little baskets in the neighborhood, and to those in Little Italy, on the other side of the main drag of town, Broad Street, and in the new village.

You could get 10¢ a basket, and what with getting upward of twelve baskets from a bucket, there was money to be made. The huckleberry season lasted only a couple of weeks, what with all those old ladies in there grabbing up so many.

Here was another vocation lesson, though I didn't view it that way since I hadn't even heard the word *vocation*: competition is a pain in the butt—especially from old ladies.

I don't remember how I found out about making costume jewelry, but I think it must have been from a comic book I had around the house. I sent away for a few things, like a magic decoder ring or a telescope that would let you see through walls and balsa wood airplane kits, so this must have been another of those things. I got an assortment of "stones": blue, red, yellow, pink, green, and in different shapes and sizes. There were mountings too: bracelets, necklaces, earrings, and hair pins. I made up a bunch of things and went house to house peddling them. This venture didn't last long. I couldn't sell much. Either they weren't pretty enough or cheap enough, or something. Besides, the money to be made wasn't nearly as good as that from selling muskrat hides or huckleberries.

*You have to know about how much money something will make before you put money into it.*

I was in the Boy Scouts for a few years and went to camp for a week each year, where we were shown crafts and outdoor stuff. They were really hobbies, like lanyards, and belts and fire making, and canoeing and swimming; but if you did the requirements, you could get a merit badge to put on your uniform.

The more badges, the higher the rank and the more respect. Ah-ha!

We held paper drives once a year. People would save their old newspapers for us. We rode around on a large stake body truck that someone loaned to us, going from house to house, and block by block, section of town by section of town. We were not told how much money came from this.

I guess we were too young to understand. I got that a lot about a lot of things.

Our town had its legal system. It was one cop car, four or five cops, and a chief of police, along with Judge Oliver "(Ollie)" Daniels. The cops would arrest someone for speeding down "New Hill" coming into town from Bridgeport, mostly with out-of-state tags, and haul them in front of Ollie, who would levy a fine. Ollie was ancient and had been that way from my earliest recollection of him. He was a Justice of the Peace (JP), not a regular Judge. Ollie was hard of hearing. When we would see a cop escorting someone to Ollie's courtroom, the front room of his house, which was alongside our hangout, "Pop's," on Broad Street, we would creep into the narrow alley between Pop's and Ollie's and peer in the window. This night provides me this memory. Ollie had been asleep; after all, it was later than eight o'clock. Ollie asked if the person wanted to plead guilty or not guilty, and the person replied, "Guilty."

Ollie leaned forward and asked again with his head turned sideways, the way people who are hard of hearing do. Again, the person answered, a little louder this time, because he noticed that Ollie was having a hard time hearing him. Ollie leaned farther forward and said, "Speak up when I ask you a question." As he was admonishing the defendant, Ollie noticed he didn't have his hearing aid turned on, so he corrected that. When the defendant answered this time, he raised his voice quite loud. Ollie snapped back into his seat as the words slammed into his hearing aid and in a very stern, indignant voice announced, "Guilty. You're guilty, and fined double for shouting in this courtroom. That'll teach you to have respect."

I saw that justice will not always be fair, although we were laughing so hard our sides hurt.

# EXPERIENCES WITH MY DAD AND MOM

The houses in the old village were offered for purchase, so those who were paying rent could have their payments applied to purchase the house. This brought about a wave of self-improvement projects. The first big projects were to put foundations under the houses since they were held up by brick piers that had begun sinking. No one could afford to pay someone to do this work, so it was always do it yourself (DIY). A couple of people chose to put a basement under their house, but my dad chose to go with just a foundation. Of course, I was drafted to help. My introduction to house construction began with this project.

The first step in construction is drawing plans. My dad had help with that from someone. Me helping meant first learning what the plans showed we had to do. A foundation required a base of concrete called a footer to go in first, then the cinder-block foundation wall on top of that, then a wooden plate to which the house would be bolted. All this was to come out at the exact same height all around the house, and level. A line level would help with that.

But before the foundation could be built, the house had to be raised off the existing piers, so we had to build pads for the jacks we'd use to raise the house. Railroad jacks, the kind used to jack up railroad cars, were used to jack up the house, so my dad and I dug holes the right depth and put thick planks in the bottom of them for the jacks to sit on. The jacks would have large wooden beams sit on them and run under the house, perpendicular to the main house support beams.

Next, we dug a trench all around, right below the edges of the house, deep enough to allow a cement footer to be poured and the block foundation and plate to fit beneath the house. We didn't give much thought to what would happen if a jack or beam slipped.

I found out that laws dictated how thick and wide the footer needed to be, and the material that needed to be used.

I learned of footers and what they did. Then foundations and what they did. Then that blocks were laid staggered half block over half block for strength. I learned how to lay out where to dig, and how far down to dig for the foundation. I learned how to cut blocks with a swift chop of a trowel after chiseling the line where the break was to be. All this came from my dad, and I have no idea where he'd gotten this knowledge.

Summer and heat and humidity and digging holes for flat wood supports that would go under the jacks all went together. Then came the leveling string stretched between sites for jacks at the exact height, which allowed for the jack, its support, and the beam that would run beneath the house, jack to jack and perpendicular to the beams holding up the house. Some of the supports were placed beyond the house by a couple of feet; others were placed under the house.

All this needed to be done before we could dig the trench for the footer, which had to be the right depth to allow for the required thickness of the footer and the block foundation and the plate that would go between the ground and the house.

*Things have to be done in order. Don't start until you know everything that has to be done.*

No machines. Shovels and backs and arms only. Digging involved being under the house, bent over, and swinging the filled shovel around to pile the dirt beyond the house. String levels and stakes were the first to go in as guides for where the flat supports for the jacks would go. There were stakes at the corners of the house out a few feet with string stretched between at the same height all the way around and running level under the house perpendicular to the beams that held the place up.

Construction work is interesting, but the physical requirement and dirt are not.

Two sand, one stone, and one cement was a formula I was taught. It's the ingredients for the concrete we mixed in a wheelbarrow with a hoe, then shoveled into buckets and poured into the foundation form we made from 2" x 4" studs. The mixture for the "mud" that was used to hold the cinder blocks in place was different, and there were no stones. *Setup time* was another term I learned. Once mixing and pouring cement was started, a whole length of footer had to be poured before any of it could be set up.

There were other cement mixing formulas for other applications. The art of laying block and brick is fascinating. It involves getting mud to just the right consistency and then putting just the right amount of mud on the block so the distance between blocks would be consistent above, below, and between, plus mixing only the amount you can use before it began to set. Each course had to be exactly the same as all others: level and plumb.

The garage project came next. Dad decided we needed one and that I should help him build it. Sixteen-inch centers and thirty-degree and forty-five-degree angles were added to what I understood. Toeing nails but not screws also got in there along with dry lumber, flat, level, plumb, and warp, all of which took on meaning.

My dad took me fishing in a place called Alloway Creek. It was out in the farm country of South Jersey. It wasn't really a successful trip as far as fish were concerned, but it was in that I learned about some other vocations. As we were riding through the countryside, we came upon a truck that was loaded with what looked like weeds piled high and hanging over the sides to dragging on the road. I learned they were pea vines. We followed the truck to a field where there was a large green machine with a spout on one end, an opening on the other, and a large piece of canvas sloped from top to bottom, end to end, between them. The truck pulled up to the chute end, and they started pitchforking the vines into the inlet. The machine vibrated and growled until peas started bouncing down the canvas into a big container. The spout on the end opposite the inlet was for discharge where all the shredded vines blew out into the bed of another truck. I was, and still am, fascinated by how that apparatus opened the pea pods and got the peas out without crushing them.

We drove some distance to another place that had a group of igloo-shaped buildings. There was a mixer-looking thing that some guy was pouring reddish-colored dirt into an end. There was an oblong-shaped discharge duct on other end of the mixer where a steady loaf-like stream of peanut butter–consistency red stuff was slowly being shoved out onto a slow-moving conveyor belt. A little way down, there was a wheel that cut across the path of the red peanut butter. The wheel had one spoke made of wire and was timed with the conveyor. The wheel turned every once in a while so the wire cut through the strip of red peanut butter mud in regular distances. The cut pieces of red mud rode the conveyor to the end, and each cut piece was lifted onto a flat slab of metal. The filled slabs were stacked on a wheeled rack that was maybe eight feet high.

Some guy pushed the rack into one of the igloo-like little houses where there was a bunch of other racks. These little houses were ovens. The red mud blocks were baked and cooled for six weeks into the red bricks that are used to make buildings.

After we saw bricks being made, we stopped at the Richmond Ice Cream Factory in Woodstown, where we saw how ice cream was made. There wasn't much to be seen since it all was in pipes and tanks, but we did see that milk and cream went in one end and flavoring and coloring went in other places. I was treated to some in the shop that was connected to the factory.

There was another local attraction in Woodstown: Cowtown. This was where livestock was auctioned and peddlers of every sort sold their wares. Some had tables inside long buildings, and some sold from tables in the open.

It was open only on Tuesdays. A lesson here was that you hardly ever got what you thought you were buying. That gold watch wasn't. That designer dress wasn't. That lifetime guarantee wasn't. But the really inexpensive clothing and other odds and ends were what you expected them to be.

I learned to trust the saying "buyer beware."

There was an auction in a separate building where the first item offered for bidding was a mystery box. The bidding was open until the price reached as high as it was going to go, then the "Sold to the lady/gentleman in the straw hat," or whatever distinguished them, was announced.

As the lucky bidder was paying, the auctioneer announced the special deal for the day: anyone who wanted to have a mystery box could step right up and get one at the same price. Then, as people were stepping up to get in on the special deal at the special price, without knowing what was in the mystery box, another item up for auction was brought out. The lucky people getting in on the special deal handed over their money but were given a number to verify they were in on the deal of the day. The mystery boxes weren't being handed out while others were still lining up to pay. The person collecting the money for the mystery boxes was called upon to take care of the person who won the bid for the next item, and the auctioneer became preoccupied with the ongoing auctioning, as did the person who was to hand out the mystery boxes. If you paid for a mystery box, you were stuck at the auction until the end, unless you were willing to forfeit your money.

Trucks filled with livestock would back up to the pens and ramps at the rear of Cowtown and were hooked up to the chutes so the animals could be unloaded. When the doors were opened, the horses, cows, or pigs were herded out and into pens, where they were going to be held until auction. I fell in the pathway once as a bunch of cattle were being unloaded. I had the fright of my life as I frantically climbed back out. The livestock auction was held in a large arena-like building. An animal with a white number painted on its side was brought in the center and driven around while the bidders who sat around the viewing area would bid. I learned what a cattle prod is. I learned what kind of person most of the people who did this kind of thing were.

My dad had been a musician before he got married. He had a fifteen-minute radio show broadcast out of City Hall in Camden near the top floor. *George Silver* was the show's name. He played his drums, whistled, and sang. He had a set of drums, snare, tom-tom, and bass. A high hat, worked from a foot pedal, and a large cymbal were fastened to the bass drum. The base drum had a silhouette picture of a Southern belle painted inside. It showed its colors when the light inside was on. He had an opportunity with his little band to go on a job on a cruise ship, but instead chose to go to work at the DuPont plant and marry my mother.

*Choosing security or ego gratification is the first choice to be made.*

Dad started teaching me to play drums from a battered old brown book. There were paradiddles and flams to get down pat and notes on paper to learn what to do with the sticks or brushes. I didn't get to use the drums themselves, only the practice board, which was a piece of rubber glued to a flat piece of wood. Two taps from one stick, then two taps of the other stick with the rapidity increasing until the flutter sound turned into almost a hum without the sound of individual sticks. He'd be in another room, and I'd hear "Your left stick is heavy" as I sat nearly bored to death trying to learn to roll. When Dad was not home, I'd sneak the drums out and try playing the set, annoying the rest of the block with the racket.

The thing that stopped that career path was a lack of rhythm.

My dad was active in St. Michael's Roman Catholic Church; Mom wasn't. He sang in the choir, and I'd sit up there during Mass. Later, I joined the choir. I learned from the nuns that my friends who went to the Methodist church across the street wouldn't be going to heaven because they weren't Catholic. Catholic was the only true Christian religion. I was told many things I didn't understand, like God always has been and always will be. This was a concept beyond my comprehension. When I'd ask questions about such things, I'd get "God works in mysterious ways. Ways beyond man's ability to understand." So I just shut up.

Dad was active in lots of things around town. There were talent shows held in the grammar school. Because my dad was an organizer and host, I was not allowed in the contest, but I got to sing by myself or with my dad as part of the show. This didn't sit very well with me, but I just shut up. I can still see the microphone as it appeared, with the strong lights shining through it, outlining the inner works. I couldn't see the audience because of the bright lights in my eyes. During a show, we were doing a duet when he started whistling. I looked over at him to see what was going on.

After the show, he told me he just wanted to see how I handled that. I did all right, I guess, since I kept on singing.

I did get into one show on my own. Spike Jones had a comedy kind of orchestra, and one of the tunes was "I'm a Lonely Little Petunia (In an Onion Patch)." My mom made a headpiece with flowers all around it so my face was in the middle. I mimed to the record, and when it came to the part "And all I did was cry all day / Boo hoo, boo hoo," I faked crying. The audience loved that part. At the height of my career, I was asked to sing at the eighth-grade commencement of the town just south of Gibbstown, Bridgeport, and that was the extent of my musical career.

My mother started a discount shoe business in our house. We lost a living room but gained a bunch of shoe racks and shoes. I'm not sure how I got involved. Most likely, I was pressed into the business. I learned about women's shoes. Sizes, pumps, flats, spikes, wedgies, open toed, closed toed, A through E widths, straps, closed heels, and colors. God, the colors! Blue wasn't blue anymore, and neither was green—green and so on. I learned the purchase of a pair of shoes wasn't simply buying a pair of shoes. There was the whole process of matching of outfits and handbags and stockings depending on the occasion. And there was "I'm just not really sure. Let me think about this awhile. I'll come back." They usually didn't.

*Another vocation lesson: close the sale.*

I went with my mother on buying trips to the wholesalers. These were big warehouses in Philadelphia, and buying involved an entire day, a long day. And bus rides. Mom didn't drive. We had only one car, and Dad used it to get to and from the plant. Words like *closeout items*, *quantity purchase*, *shipping*, *discounts* became part of my language. And there were whispered exchanges between my mom and the warehouse guy about something when I was out of earshot. I think there was some friction between my mother and my father, but I wasn't really aware of it, or I chose not to pay attention.

Next came moving the store out of the house and into an actual shop.

> I learned about growth, location, availability, and advertising.

There was a vacant storefront up in Greens. That was another part of town, above the grammar school and below Ashton's Bend. For such a small town, there were certainly a lot of different names of sections. The landlord I remember. He didn't have a hair on his body that I could see. I was told he had some disease that made all his hair fall out. And his car—oh! His car. It was a Packard, an old humpback thing, and the body wasn't right. It didn't line up. The front wheels weren't directly in front of the rear wheels. It rolled down the street sort of like a crab walks.

The shoe store went on from there out until my mother decided to become a beautician (hairdresser) and opened that kind of shop. My mother was an adventurous sort, always looking for ways to bring in some money. I guess she just wasn't satisfied with being a housewife. I was in the Air force by that time and didn't have anything to do with it.

I had a cousin, fourth or fifth or something, who owned a couple of deep-sea fishing boats in Stone Harbor. The boats were named *Alwin* and *Irwin*, as were my cousins. My dad took me there a couple of times. Cutting bait, preparing fishing lines, outriggers, bottom fishing, and trolling became things I knew about; so did seasickness. So long as the boat was moving I was fine. When the anchor hit the water, I hit the rail, and stayed there. A sailor I was not going to be, although what I was going to be hadn't even entered my mind yet.

We had an electric washing machine that was a tub-like thing with a wringer over the tub so water could be squeezed from the clothes. I got my fingers squashed more than once when I was not paying close-enough attention to what I was doing. First, the wash water was poured in, and the clothes were washed. Then the water was drained, and clean rinse water was put in. The clothes were rinsed and squeezed, and then the water was drained. It was a lot of work. We wanted a clothes washer, but before we could do that, we had to have a place to put it. Dad decided to add a room to the house. We were going to move the heater and the washer into the new utility room.

The house heater was a coal-fired thing, and the heating system was hot water. Water ran through the heat exchanger part of the coal-fired heater, which looked like the radiators throughout the house (only a lot bigger), then out through the hot water pipe up into the hot water tank that was in an upstairs bedroom. There was another section of the coal-fired heater that supplied the hot water tank where water was stored for bathing and cleaning.

I learned what a closed system was. All the pipes and the water tank upstairs were filled and closed off. The hot water wanted to rise to the top, and the cold water wanted to fall to the bottom, where the heater was. The water circulated through the house that way. A leaky pipe was a disaster.

My job was to shake down the ashes in the heater into a coal bucket, take them outside, and dump them into an ash bin. I filled the coal bucket from the coal shed, which was a little tin building by the alley out back and returned the filled bucket to the house.

Each house had a coal shed on the alley. Munyan's coal delivery truck would come down the alley, and the driver would swing a chute around to the window of the shed and lift the bed of the truck until a section of the truck would empty into our coal shed. Each section of the truck held a ton of coal. The clatter of coal rattled the whole neighborhood. We bought coal by the ton or half ton.

On my way to grammar school, I'd pass Munyan's coal yard. New coal arriving was a spectacle to behold. There was a ramp that ran on an angle from the back of Munyan's property, a couple of stories above the ground, past the office out to the street. A large truck with coal piled high above the sides would be driven half a block up the street, the driver would hang out of the door, and then, looking back, he'd gun the engine to a roar, and the truck would get up ahead of speed so it could make it up the ramp onto the short area at the top where it was flat, then slam on the brakes to stop before it reached the end of the ramp. I used to think the driver was a daredevil guy. The truck would dump its load of coal on the pile beneath it and then ease its way back down the ramp, brakes hissing all the way. They filled delivery trucks from this pile.

The alley was our connection to the delivery and tradesmen of the world. Coal men delivered coal, trash men picked the trash, garbage men picked up garbage, junk men picked up junk. The sound of "RAGS, RAGS" bounced off all the houses when he was in the alley. Salesmen arrived at the front of the house.

The utility room became where clothes were washed and ironed. They were hung outside to dry. In winter, the clothes would freeze stiff or were hung inside.

We switched from coal to oil heat, and the coal shed became something different. It became Dad's workshop and was the place where I learned about a table saw, drill press, and grinder wheels along with a myriad of tools. It was also where I learned not to push what I was cutting on the table saw toward the blade with my fingers in line with the blade. The end of my finger still shows signs of the scar.

# LIFE WITH FRIENDS

I graduated from Greenwich Township Public School in 1953.

The shed became the place where we'd play a card game similar to 21 (blackjack) for pennies, only the goal was 7½. It was where I learned friends will cheat you for money. It was much later that I learned my run of bad luck wasn't really luck at all.

We, my friends and I, took to hanging out on the main corner of town: the crossing of Repauno Avenue and Broad Street, in front of Pop's Restaurant. Across the street was the town gas station, which was a convenient place for the police to sit in their car waiting for unlawful things to happen. There was one policeman who had the idea he was a jackbooted storm trooper or something. He'd been in the Korean police action, as that war was called. His treatment of us was not appreciated. Other cops would tell us to get off the street, and we'd just move to another corner; but the way this cop did the same thing came off all wrong. This cop also thought he was a Don Juan. He ended up getting one of the waitresses pregnant.

The police car would be parked in the driveway of the gas station after closing for the night, no matter which policeman was on duty. One of them left it there practically all evening: Super Cop. He'd turn the radio up loud and leave the door open while he was in Pop's smoozing the waitresses. Temptation being what it was and we becoming who we were becoming, a couple of us stood in front of the window blocking the view of the police car while one of us sneaked across the street and pushed the door of the police car closed with the lock button pushed down. Later, when Pop's closed, the cop came out to get into his car. No go! He nearly exploded, yelling and threatening us with all manner of bad things. We put on our most innocent faces and told him how sorry we were for his problem. He went to someone's house nearby and called the chief of police, who soon arrived with the only other set of keys. They were two very unhappy policemen, one more than the other.

A person would think that someone subjected to such a trick would learn from it.

There came another night when Super Cop was in Pop's romancing the waitresses and not paying attention. The police car was in its usual place, only this time, he had another set of keys with him. He had begun making a big show of that, along with his superior attitude as he strutted by us. When the situation was right, two of us went in to Pop's and sat in a booth in the back. Super Cop sat staring at us in his super cop attitude while we watched the police car being pushed around behind the gas station behind his back. The other guys came into Pop's, and we all filled the back booths. The stare down continued for another half hour or so until Super Cop suddenly realized his police car wasn't were he left it. In a rage, he stormed out, and then back in. He began threatening us with bodily harm. This went on for a while until he called the chief on the store phone to report the car stolen and threatening us with life in prison, or worse.

Before the chief came to Pop's, he called the state police because they didn't have a police vehicle to answer any calls.

The Staties arrived with lights flashing, and questions were asked all round. We informed the Staties we had been in Pop's and had no idea what happened to his police car. All the off-duty police officers were called, and more Staties showed up. The area was filled with flashing police car lights.

A search for the missing car was begun, and cops went off in all directions. When one of the last Staties was leaving to go in the opposite direction of the others, he circled around the gas station. He walked back, stood by the gas pumps, and called the chief over. They both went behind the station. The chief slowly drove the missing police car around to the front of the station. Super Cop lost his job.

*Policemen/women aren't always what they are supposed to be.*

We had a twice per year ritual at our house. In the fall it was when the screens on the porch and all the windows were exchanged for storm windows and the opposite in the spring. There were no storm windows on the porch. There was installing new screens and puttying the storm windows before they were put in. New screens had to be done every year due to the corrosive air quality that dissolved them to the point they crumbled at a touch. We stored the storm windows and screens over the rafters in the garage. Cutting screens and putting wire brads through ¼" half round molding to hold glass and screen was time consuming. Making the frames required cutting forty-five-degree cuts, which matched up to ninety-degree corners. Cutting glass required scoring the glass with a glass cutter and then carefully tapping it over an edge of something so it would break along the score.

*Making and repairing things can be interesting but tedious.*

There were two movie theaters in Paulsboro. Gibbstown didn't have any. One was the Hill, and for some reason, we called the other one the Bang-Bang. Parents and older people went to the Hill; kids went to the Bang-Bang. Black kids sat in the balcony. When the lights went down and it got dark in the Bang-Bang, just before the curtain was opened and the screen lit up the place, the noise level rose to a din so loud you couldn't hear the movie sounds. It got so dark your eyes had to adjust before you could see anything.

In those few moments, when the show was about to start, one of us sitting in the front row would sneak through the curtain at the emergency exit beside the stage and open the back door. The kids who didn't have money for a ticket would rush in. Matinees were a problem since sunlight would stream in when the door was opened.

I couldn't hear much of the movie sound since the din continued all through the showing. I didn't like the Bang-Bang very much, but it was the Saturday-afternoon thing to do and where the "in crowd" went. And there were the serials where, at the last minute, the hero, Hop-along Cassidy, Gene Autry, Tom Mix would come up with some new twist and win over the bad guy. The bad and good guys were easy to pick out because the good guy always wore a white hat and the bad guy wore a black one; same for the color of the horses. It never occurred to us that hiding behind a turned-up card table when being shot at with pistols from twenty feet away wouldn't really protect a person, or to count the number of shots taken with a six-shooter. In retrospect, I think they were hundred-shooters.

The people who owned the theaters didn't do a very good job of making sure they were paid by everyone who attended. They lost money every performance, but I didn't notice, or care.

Our transportation to the movies was always by thumbing rides up and back between Gibbstown and Paulsboro. Kids coming home would collect on one of three corners and leave in small groups and squeezed as many as they could into whichever car would stop.

There weren't any girls, but we didn't notice. They just weren't there.

There was a funeral parlor a block down from the Hill, and we'd check the basement windows to see if there was any activity going on. There were two reasons: we might see a naked woman, and we could see blood being drained from the bodies. After seeing a vampire movie, this added to our night of fright. "Eeww" is how we described what the person doing the embalming was doing. Creepy!

After the war ended, train cars loaded with expended shells were pulled through town. There were cannon shells and containers filled with machine gun and rifle shells all piled high in open gondola cars. On occasion, some shells that were a mystery and big—we called them torpedoes—showed up.

You could raise a little money from selling things like tin cans, metal, and rags that used to be junk. We knew the trash man would pay for metal. Brass and copper would bring the most money. And here were thousands of brass things moving right past our houses! The train men knew this cargo was liable to be stolen, so they never stopped the train and thought that took care of preventing theft. Maybe three-quarters of a mile from Repauno Avenue, there was a dirt hill built so Broad Street could cross over the railroad tracks on a bridge high enough for the train to go beneath the road (we called that "New Hill"). The train didn't stop but had to slow down at that crossing by Billy Burt's. The train man needed time to get to the crossing to stop the automobiles by waving his lantern and flag. Once the engine was on the crossing, the train man jumped back on the engine.

Trains ran on a reliable schedule, pretty much; so on the day the shell train, as we called it, was to get to Gibbstown, we'd go down to 'new hill' and wait for it to arrive. When the engine approached and slowed in preparation for crossing Repauno Avenue, there was a long line of loaded gondola cars strung out from New Hill to Repauno Avenue. We'd jump the cars, which were moving past New Hill and the field by the new VFW. There'd be one of us on each end of about five cars. We'd climb in and start throwing shells overboard and keep throwing shells until we got to about a block from my house, then we'd jump off. By that time, the train had picked up enough speed that we had to get off anyway. We had shells strewn all along the railroad tracks from New Hill to the digger hole. This was where the rainwater culvert for the old village emptied at the railroad and where we'd play with our toy cars.

We could hide a couple of shells in our coal sheds, but someone would find them if we left them there for too long. We learned there was a federal law against what we were doing, but the money was good. For a while, we sold our brass shells to the junk man; but then suddenly, he wasn't so eager to buy them. We heard the FBI was snooping around.

We had a product storage problem.

We all were pretty good at jumping the train, but one guy, Lou from Paulsboro, had an accident. I wasn't there and don't know why he was jumping a train, maybe just to ride it, but he wasn't jumping the shell train with us. The way I heard it, his foot missed the lowest rung of the ladder, and he fell, one leg across the tracks, under the train. Before he could recover, the train wheel cut off his leg. In shock, he reached for his leg and that arm was cut off, too. We'd always been warned not to jump trains. I remember, some years later, helping Lou wash his hand.

On the end of my street, Logan Avenue, opposite from the railroad, there was a line of garages people could rent. This was before my dad built our own garage. The dad of one of the members of our gang of shell collectors rented a garage but didn't use it for their car. Hawk: whose real name was Howard and a grade or two ahead of us and more ambitious than most, stashed his shells in his dad's garage and had a bunch of them in there. He threw all that he could from every train. The rest of us just didn't throw any more than we could hide and sell.

We sacrificed the money we could make for the safety of not getting caught.

Selling shells came to an end for two reasons: Hawk's shells were discovered in the garage, and the trains stopped coming through town.

As long as I'm speaking of the garages: one sunny day, my attention was drawn to another exciting event that sometimes happened in my town. The bell at the firehouse rang. I ran for my bicycle so I could follow the truck to see what was causing the excitement. Turned out the fire trucks were coming toward me. The garages were on fire. I saw the firemen, in their raincoats and hip boots and fireman's hard hat, go to work unloading hoses and hooking them up to fire hydrants, and banging the sides of garages open with axes and trying to get stuff out of them. It was really hot that day, and they were sweating before they even got off the fire truck. My dad ran up, unlocked our garage, and drove our car out. The fire was toward the other end of the line of garages, so he could do that.

Firemen had to be ready to run at the clang of the bell, any time of day, any day, and deal with roaring fires.

My sister suffered from epilepsy. One day I found her lying on the dining room floor having a seizure, and knowing only what I'd seen people do on TV in that situation, I threw a glass of water on her. It snapped her out of it, but I was roundly instructed that was the wrong thing to do.

I don't like seeing people in distress and recoil from it. The Medical field is not for me.

Once I got to be fourteen years old, I could work for farmers at harvest time. New Jersey was called The Garden State mainly because the whole of South Jersey was farm land. I lived right next to tomato country. Del Monte Foods had a tomato processing plant in Swedesboro, which is right in tomato country. The thing about tomatoes is that one plant will produce tomatoes for several weeks during harvest time, so one field can be harvested a lot of times. I got a job picking tomatoes.

We kids would go to the farmhouse just outside of Bridgeport, and the farmer would take us to the field that was to be picked. There were a lot of Puerto Rican men there. The farmers built crummy little shacks the "Ricans" lived in. Not even running water. Those guys would come here for the picking season and work really long days while the season lasted. The foreman was from Puerto Rico too, but he lived here all year round and was mean to them. He took some of the money they earned. We were paid 10 cents a basket. I don't know what they were paid.

We were dropped off at the end of a row and baskets were dropped off every so often along the rows. These tomatoes weren't for market; these were for canning, so we didn't have to be very selective about which ones we'd pick: just not green and not rotten. We started very early in the morning and stayed at it until some hours later when the farmer came to collect filled baskets and take us to the barn where we could eat lunch.

The last day I had this job, we became bored with picking tomatoes. I was leaning over picking when a tomato hit my head. I looked around and saw everyone was busy picking, looking innocent. I went back to picking, and another tomato hit the other side of my body. Same thing, everyone was busy and innocent. I chose one guy and let one go in his direction. It didn't take long before we were all covered with tomatoes and there weren't many full baskets. When the farmer came to get us for lunch, he took it all in but didn't say anything. In the barn, one of us sat on the seat of a big tractor and fooled around with the pedals and levers. The thing started and moved toward a wall where window frames were leaning. He yelled that he didn't know how to stop it. A farm hand dashed in and saved most of the windows. As far we were concerned, that was why it was the last day we had a job.

Farmers stopped hiring kids as pickers around that time. They hired more "Ricans."

There were bowling alleys in the DuPont Club. Jobs as pinsetters were available and paid by the club for each ticket we got from bowlers for setting a game. I tried that for a while, but there were some hazards in that, which I didn't care for. The women bowlers were fun to set pins for. The bowling balls that some of them threw came so slowly you could count the times the ball rolled over on the way to the pins—*clump, clump, clump, clump*—and the pins seemed to topple over in slow motion. We'd catch those balls as they fell off the alley. The men were different. As soon as you'd get the pins set, you'd jump up on the divider between the alleys to get out of the way. There

were a couple of them who would throw the second ball of a turn as soon as they got it back, so we started setting the pins before we sent their ball back. If you spun the ball backward when you pushed it down the return tracks, the ball wouldn't make it up the other end, and the guy would have to walk down the alley to get it, giving us more time to set pins. We did that as a hint. It got so some of them wouldn't wait for their ball to return before they took their second shot, and a couple of us nearly got hurt. Our complaints fell on the deaf ears of one or two of them. We stopped setting for them. Another reason I stopped setting pins was that the pins would seem to explode, apart from how hard the balls hit them. They'd crash against the walls of the pit and go clear into another pit at times.

All in all the risks involved didn't seem worth ten cents a ticket.

I had what was called a cowlick in my hair. That was a tuft of hair at the back of my head that just wouldn't lie down, and it drove my sister crazy. It was like Alfalfa of *Our Gang*. She did all kinds of things to keep it down.

There were two gymnasiums in the club. There was a weight room behind one, and they would set up a boxing ring in there sometimes. I tried my hand at prizefighting. The gloves were almost like pillows; they were so large. I drew Denny Remus for my bout. I held my left hand out straight, right in front of his face; and when he'd lean over to see around it, I'd punch him in the nose. The bout was over pretty fast, and I was the winner. I won a boxing match and felt like a big shot. When I got home, I bragged to my sister, and as I was doing that, she reached over and took out the bobby pin she had holding my cowlick down. I was mortified!

I never stepped into a ring again.

*First experiences can have a lasting effect.*

A rite of passage came with seventh grade: we could write with pen and ink. That was like fifth grade when we could wear long pants. Before that, it was shorts or jodhpurs.

It was also when Roland Neal joined my class. He was a black kid, and he'd been attending our school as long as I had—only, the black kids had Mrs. Smith, who taught a special class just for them.

In the years before seventh grade, the boys shared a learning experience. During recess, we'd hear "Fight! Fight!" once in a while. It was us establishing the pecking order among us, where you learned that a bigger kid could take what he wanted. If a bigger kid wanted a lick from your ice cream cone, you'd be better off giving it to him since he'd just take it away if he wanted. And if you tried to stop him, during the tussle, the ice cream would likely end on the ground, so neither of you got any. This ritual pretty much stopped once we started getting big enough to really hurt each other. Hawk got into a fight with somebody, and the sound of fists landing on one's face turned out to be a deterrent. You had to have a good reason to get into a fight from then on.

Power and strength established our pecking order, and that order remained respected.

Gibbstown, Bridgeport, and Repaupo didn't have a high school. We were bussed to Paulsboro.

Some of the older kids were getting driver's licenses, and our attention turned to cars. The fad of the day was modifying older cars, and the '40 Ford coupes were the hot item, and plentiful. Cars weren't built during the war; all that manufacturing capacity was taken for war vehicles. The new cars were the preferred cars, and that left the old '40 Fords at the bottom of the market. Modifying was done by de-chroming, painting with gray primer, and shackling the rear springs down so the car rode front end high. This didn't cost much money since it was DIY. We'd chip in to buy a couple of gallons of gas for Tony's car and go off to Westville, or the other direction to Pennsville. When we got there, we did the same thing we did in front of Pop's. We loitered and made remarks we thought were smart to different girls. We'd discovered girls but weren't sure what we were to do with them. We had an idea that came from little eight-page books we got from the barbershop. And 8mm films, which were the pornography of the time that were shown at "smokers." The local boys didn't appreciate us, so we ended up getting into fistfights. This led to belts with the buckles sharpened, which we'd wrap around our hands and use as weapons. Stilettos showed up too, and there was even a zip gun. We'd discovered the radio antenna on a car was just the right size for a .22 caliber bullet to fit in; and with a little work, you could craft a wood stock with a rubber band firing pin. A zip gun was what we called it.

This was the beginning of box-toed shoes, white T-shirts with the sleeves rolled up, and dungarees folded up in narrow turns so they were pegged tightly at the ankle. And the ducktail haircut, where we had our hair long, combed back, and in the back we swept the hair up and dragged a finger down where the hair from the sides met so there was a sort of wave. Marlon Brando dressed like that in his movies.

The night before Halloween, Mischief Night, was the night we looked for naughty things to do. Naughty doesn't really capture the spirit. Year to year, we graduated from fun, annoying things, to destructive things as we attempted to outdo each other. We roamed the streets, staying out of sight of the cops. Dashing around, dodging the cop car was exciting in itself.

In Little Italy, there were houses without running water, and they had outhouses. On Mischief Night, we'd sneak around over there and push over outhouses. We'd only get a couple, but the excitement buildup was intense. There was one that no one had ever gotten. It was "*the* one to get," so we decided this was the year. Earlier that night, we'd picked a garage up in Greens that we'd noticed was leaning a lot—propped up with boards—asking to be pushed over, so we did. We ran all the way back to Pop's. While I was running, I noticed a line of clothes hanging in a backyard. You just didn't do that on Mischief Night. I went back and cut the whole line down, then took it to the post office and ran it up the flagpole. The whole town saw the ladies' unmentionables dangling in the breeze the next morning.

The Mancinelli's' outhouse was guarded by old man Mancinelli. He'd sit in the kitchen with the lights out, holding a shotgun loaded with rock salt. Old man Mancinelli made sure everyone knew he was there. Rock salt's the same stuff farmers used when guarding their pumpkin and watermelon patches.

We sneaked between the houses from the opposite block, up to the rear of Mancinelli's house. It took us quite a while to work our way to the outhouse. One guy stayed as a lookout on the side street, where he could see the back of Mancinelli's house. There were bushes and trees and briars back there, and it was dark. Four of us started pushing on the outhouse, trying to be quiet. It was heavy and hard to move. We'd push, then relax and listen for the old man, then push again. It began to move. It tilted up a few inches, and the next push would be it. We were standing in a briar bush that was sticking to us. As we started the big push, the guy next to me leaned down to pull the briars off his legs. He saw the outhouse was going to go over and reached to shove too.

His timing was off. The outhouse reached its balance point and went over just as he was reaching for it. With nothing to stop his reach, he fell forward—and in. Along with the crash of the outhouse, there was a *splush* sound. We heard the back door of the house bang open and dashed away in the direction we'd come. We met a couple of blocks over where it was safe. Do we go get him? Did he get caught? The lookout told us the old man had run back into the house yelling, and we were the only ones who ran out. We realized he was still in the outhouse, with the god-awful sewage stuff. We found this to be extremely funny. Much later, we sneaked back and helped him out. He did really stink. We hosed him off at Denny's house.

My first day at high school set the tone for me. The fad of the day was cleats on the heels of your shoes to lessen the wear, but it also gave a distinguished sound when you walked. Kind of like the sound a cowboy's spurs made in the movies. All the freshmen were in the auditorium to receive their homeroom assignments. As your name was called, you went to a section of the auditorium. I was to leave where I was seated—in the back, on the side—and go to the front on the other side. I walked across the auditorium in the area between the front and rear sections. For some reason, I think it was because my name was alphabetically toward the bottom of the list. I was the only one going to their section at the moment. The sound of my cleats on the concrete floor seemed really loud, and everyone turned to look. Clink, clink, shuffle, and clink. Clink, clink, shuffle, and clink I went. As with all auditoriums, the floor of the front section sloped toward the stage. When I took my first step on the sloped area, my cleat hit first, of course, and skidded. My foot went out from under me, and I landed on my backside. The place exploded in laughter. I was mortified.

*The difference between a cool guy and clown can be very small.*

I went out for wrestling since that was the big sport for the high school. The first day, we all did the mainstay of the training: we ran the stairs. That was the last day I was on the wrestling team. Thirty minutes of running up and down the three flights of stairs hurt everything, including my lungs, and that was why it was the last day of the wrestling team.

I didn't like gym class. It wasn't gym itself; it was showering after. And it wasn't showering—it was getting my ass snapped with towels and being pushed into lockers and other kinds of things. The bigger kids did that to us smaller kids. I was kind of tall, but skinny. There was one group of about five black kids who were all bigger. I think it was because they were all older, from staying back several grades in grammar school. The lesson I'd learned in grammar school told me to shut up and take it, so I did—almost. Fights in high school were usually challenge kinds of things that started with, "I'll meet you after school." I avoided confrontation with every one of the black kids from gym. I even went the long way from class to class to avoid being in the same hallway with them.

There was one guy more my age and size who hung around with the bunch of bigger black kids. He decided to pick on me too. He said, or did, something that I don't remember, but he didn't have size on me and wasn't surrounded by his friends. I was not going to take it, and I shouted, right there in the hallway, "I'll see you after school." The hallway got really quiet. I was a nervous wreck the rest of the afternoon. I was asked over and over if I was really going to meet that guy after school. I was there, waiting. He didn't show up, and I was glad he didn't. The guys in gym class didn't snap my ass anymore, and I wasn't pushed out of line at the gym door anymore.

*You not standing up for you can hurt more and a lot longer than standing up for yourself.*

Just over New Hill, toward Bridgeport, there were three ditches that carried water to the riverbank. We called them First Ditch, Second Ditch, and Third Ditch. I didn't know what the real names were. They were in that order south from Gibbstown for about a mile or so toward Bridgeport. All three were too deep to walk across and were about twelve to twenty feet wide, just enough so we couldn't get across them. The second and third ditches were south of the DuPont fence and farthest from Gibbstown. Second Ditch was the most navigable and straight all the way to the bank of the river. It was the one we used to boat to the river. First Ditch was navigable only to the Dupont fence, and beyond that it spread out into what we called Magazine Lake. We called it that because it separated all the storage magazines with the explosives in them. There was a small branch ditch that we called Frog Ditch that opened into marsh just before the fence. All the area around Magazine Lake was wooded and marshy. You couldn't see but a few yards, and then only along the path of the tracks.

Access to Frog Ditch and one bank of First Ditch was from the Gibbstown side of New Hill, the Old Village side; and access to the other side of First Ditch was on the Bridgeport side of New Hill. You could only get to the Bridgeport side of First Ditch, and back to the fence, from the south side of New Hill: First Ditch and the railroad tracks effectively isolated Frog Ditch. We knew this, but no one else did. This became important when we started Night Ducking.

The Plant was like a large game preserve, since it was fenced in. I was doing a lot of hunting through those years. Both shotgun and bow and arrow. I hunted rabbit, squirrel, ducks, pheasants, and some deer.

Ducks started looking for a feeding and resting place for the night around dusk, so that's when we went ducking. It was against the law to have firearms in the woods after sunset, but we'd begun paying attention only to laws we might get caught breaking.

Explosives were stored in large magazines along both sides of Magazine Lake. The railroad tracks, which were used to transport the explosives to and from the magazines, made great paths for getting back to Magazine Lake and the many magazines. We simply jumped the fence at Frog Ditch and walked all the way to the magazines and the riverbank, protected from game wardens by the fence. The tracks turned to cross Magazine Lake out of sight from the road that came in from the south side of New Hill.

We entered Frog Ditch from the A Line road entrance to the plant. We didn't cross the railroad tracks by my house and walk on the road or railroad in the open. Instead, we went through the woods down by the huckleberry patch. We entered the woods by crossing the tracks a block down from my house. We were only in the open a short time. We walked to the fence through the woods and climbed over it. From there, it was a clear walk to Magazine Lake. The return way was the reverse of the way in. Since we'd wait until three thirty or four in the afternoon, all the activity in the magazine area was done for the day, and the game wardens weren't allowed on the property. We stood there, sometimes on top of the explosives, to shoot at the ducks.

The game wardens followed the sound of our shotguns from the road between Gibbstown and Bridgeport and entered the woods from the Bridgeport side of New Hill and First Ditch. That put First Ditch and the fence between us and them. It took a couple of years before the game wardens found our side of First Ditch and stationed themselves along the A Line railroad tracks. They weren't waiting for us every day, and we were never sure if they were waiting for us. We stayed in the woods every time, and we were silent on the way out. One of us walked ahead a short distance and was either singing or whistling all the way out. If he stopped singing or whistling, we stopped moving until he started again. We had his gun and ducks, so as far as the game wardens could prove, he was just out walking in the woods in the dark. It was brazen but effective.

The place we came out of the woods was on the opposite side of the woods from where the game wardens would be waiting on the tracks, and it was only a short distance from there to home.

I learned about being quiet in the woods while squirrel hunting. There was a small feeder ditch to the first ditch, where there was an opening in the trees and squirrels returning to their nests would jump from tree to tree to cross over the ditch. I'd take up a position and wait there for them. I was totally silent and could hear the sounds of the woods and noticed that all the animals and birds would jump as they moved about on the ground, so there was the sound they made, and then quiet, when they could listen for other sounds. Some friends came through where I was hunting, and the amount of racket they made as they shuffled through the dried leaves and twigs was staggeringly loud. No wonder we had such a hard time getting game! I walked deliberately, picking my feet straight up and putting them straight down from then on.

One evening, as I sat waiting for squirrels, an owl flew so close to my head I felt the breeze from his wings on my face—but not a sound. He was completely silent in flight. I learned later that an owl's feathers do not have the serrated edges that other birds' feathers have, so: silent flight. I watched another one, another time, as he was hunting too. He turned his head almost completely around. Their eyes are fixed; they don't move. Huh!

Despite this upland game knowledge, I didn't see this leading to a job.

We spent that year having great fun being pranksters. There were many times when I was home alone and we'd gather at my house. Other times, we'd go over to the train station and drink the gallon of beer we'd buy for $1 at the back door of Billy's. Other nights, when my mother was home, we'd wait until she was in bed and then push the car out of the garage into the alley. We'd go for a joy ride. One night we went out of town toward Swedesboro, through Repaupo.

I had it floored as we went through Repaupo. We knew there weren't any cops out there. One of the kids from there was telling a story about a car that flew through Repaupo. They heard the car coming and were convinced it was not going to make the curve and there was going to be a crash. When the car rounded the bend, it was leaning so far over that the side dug a little furrow along the side of the road. We came really close to an early end that night.

Gibbstown didn't have any taxicabs, but Paulsboro did. There was a phone on the bank corner, and the cabs would wait in line there. We called for a cab to come to Logan Avenue, then waited five minutes and called for another, then did it again until no one answered the phone. We sat in my dark house watching cabs roam up and down and listening to the cab drivers swearing at every house on the block.

Another night, we called the mortuary in Paulsboro and asked if someone could come to pick up Mr. Bill Ellis on Logan Avenue. When the hearse turned onto the street, we were ducking down, holding our sides and trying not to be heard. The man knocked on the door, and Lizzie Ellis answered. We couldn't hear what he said, but we sure did hear her when she screamed, "Get down here so this guy can see you're not dead."

One night we found bundles of burlap on the deck of the train station. It took work, but with some rope and effort, we put the bundles on the roof of the station. For two days, there were men wearing suits. We heard they were FBI guys, wandering around over there trying to figure out how and why those bundles were up there. And for heaven's sake, who would do such a thing?

I hitchhiked to Philly and found Professor Bremen's tattoo parlor I'd heard of from other guys. I was getting carded for beer when I was nearly forty, so you can guess how young I looked at fifteen. The place had a screen door, and the professor told us to go away after I told him I was twenty-one. I told him we'd come all the way from Gibbstown, and that unlocked the door. I chose a ribbon with a rose on it and my name in the ribbon. The other guys had just their name and high enough on their shoulder that the sleeve of their T-shirt would hide it. Not me.

My last Mischief Night, we piled some railroad ties across the road that ran behind the school. The police car came slowly up the street as we hid on the little hill across from our prank. Good thing it was a cop, and only prowling, because he could stop before hitting the ties. They were very dark, and so was the night. Anyone else could have had a pretty bad accident. Later that night, we bent over some street signs.

We ended up in front of a judge (not Ollie), and he suggested we get into the military before we ended up in the home for juvenile delinquents. I spent more days playing hooky than in class my freshman year, and I didn't get promoted. There wasn't any punishment that I remember.

My memory of the second year of high school was my dad taking me from room to room so I could return my books as I quit school. Mr. Ridenger, my algebra teacher, was the only person who tried to talk me out of it.

My friend Mel and I and I went looking for a job. We found one at the Del Monte plant in Swedesboro. They made tin cans there. The kinds that have rippled sides, and you get tomato sauce or pineapple juice in. There was a metal press machine in one corner of a huge building. It chopped off pieces of metal from flat plates, and they went into a machine that put the ripples in and soldered the bottom and sides closed. The cans were then sent up to the top of the building onto a conveyor that ran all the way around that big place up close to the ceiling to the other side, where we were stationed. When the cans reached where we were working, they were guided down on their side with the open top pointing toward us. They hit a stop and sat there in a line, looking at us. We had a rake with fifteen tines sticking straight out, like a fork. Our job was to stick the tines into the cans, lift the rake up so the cans stayed on, then turn around and put the cans onto a pallet.

The pallet was on its side like a U-shaped box so the pallet became the side of the box. The trick was to keep the rake angled enough, and to move quickly enough so that when you reached down to put the cans into the box, they wouldn't fall off the rake. There was a real knack to this, and in the beginning, we'd let one slide off the tine a lot and stand up instead of lie on its side. The box was deep enough that we couldn't reach the ill-placed can. This was a continuous operation. The metal punch press kept banging them out, and the line of cans kept moving around the building. Panic is a good way to describe our reaction when we had a misplaced can. While we were trying to get the can upright, we could see the line of stopped cans moving toward the punch press. When it reached there, the whole place was shut down, and everyone went into screaming mode. Our challenge was to get the blankety-blank can to lie down as quickly as possible.

I'd been given an aptitude test before getting the job, and I aced it. It had nothing to do with loading cans onto pallets. The person who administered the test was very impressed.

> *There is a great difference between knowing something and doing something.*

# JOINING THE AIR FORCE

If you were drafted into the military, it was two years in a foxhole getting shot at, according to our way of thinking. Jerry was sent to Valley Forge Military School by his dad. I lost touch with the rest of them except for Mel.

Mel and I decided to get as far away from foxholes as we could. I opted for the air force, and Mel went navy.

I don't remember how I got to San Antonio, Texas, but it was not by flying. My first clear recollection was of being hustled out of a bus, in the middle of the night, and told to stand at attention. We did the best we knew. Someone came around and counted us off into groups, and then we were herded into a barracks. It was a one-story affair, open bay, with beds, a thin mattress rolled up, and a blanket and sheets on top. The lights were single bulb things, harsh and glaring. There was a big box, footlocker I learned, at the foot of each bed.

I'll bring you up to speed on the tone of the place. It was 1956; the Korean police action had paused through negotiation but not ended. As of this writing, it still hasn't ended. The Army Air Corps had been turned into the United States Air Force in 1948, and General Curtis Lemay was the guy running it.

During the Korean conflict, there was an air force base named Kempo. The marines had wrested it away from the Chinese and North Koreans and turned it over to the air force. The Chinese and the North Koreans took it back from the Air Force. The marines took it back again at much loss of men and material.

I was shipped off to Lackland Air Force Base in San Antonio, Texas, for basic training and learned that General Lemay and everyone above airman last class, as we were called, were not going to have the kind of air force that required the marines to protect us. Like the navy. We were trained more along the lines of marines than airmen.

A group of about eight spiffy-looking airmen came into the barracks. One of them told us to stand at attention by a bunk. Now I knew what the beds were called. We lined up and did what we thought was attention. One of the spiffy guys told us they were our tactical instructors (TIs). They walked up and down, looking at us as though they were looking into a toilet.

Airman Second Class Whitson stepped up to the first guy in line. Not in front of him, mind you, just off his shoulder to the side, about two inches from his face. He shouted, "Where you from?" "Chicago" the guy said. Airman Second Class Whitson punched him in the stomach so hard it knocked him off his feet, and then stepped up to the next guy in line: "Where you from?"

"New Jersey."

Airman Second Class Whitson threw another god-awful punch to the stomach that knocked that guy down too. Airman Second Class Whitson strutted back to the front of the barracks. "The first word out of your mouth will be *sir*."

He walked up to the next guy in line and stared at him a few moments. Then in a softer tone of voice, he said, "So what's your name?" The guy replied, "Charles." And another punch, and another guy down.

He stepped up to the next guy. "Your name?"

"Sir, my name is Peter."

I was next in line. "Where you from?" barked Airman Second Class Whitson.

"Sir, I'm from New Jersey."

He continued through everyone else. No one else got punched. This was corporal punishment training style, we later learned.

One of the first things we were told was if we didn't like the training and decided to go AWOL (absent without official leave), we could run for two days and they could still see us—the terrain in that part of Texas was that flat.

At one point during our six weeks of basic training, Airman Second Class Whitson told us that if we ever got into a shooting war and were told to attack an enemy, if we attacked, there would be a chance we might get shot by the enemy. But if we didn't attack, it would be absolutely certain we would be shot because he would be behind us and would shoot us. We believed him.

I quickly learned one secret to not getting punched: say only—yes sir, no sir, or no excuse sir, anything other than that lead down a path to a punch. An exchange would go like this. Airman Second Class Whitson says: "You know *mumble*. You say, "Sir, I didn't hear what you said, sir." He'd say, "I said what you needed to hear, didn't I?" You reply, "Sir, no sir." He'd say, "You call me a liar, scumbag?" You: "Sir, no sir." Him: "What is your problem, numb nut?" Punch, and down you go.

*Recognize unreasonable supervisors and never challenge them.*

We would march everywhere, and we learned the dirt around there wasn't dirt—it was clay. When it rained, which it rarely did, the clay got to be like glue. First step and the clay stuck to your shoe. A big glob of clay pulled up and left a hole where you had stepped. The second step, more clay came up; third step was a surprise step. Sometimes more clay that felt like fifty pounds stuck to your foot; other times the whole glob broke loose, and your foot flew up so you nearly lost your balance. When we got to where we were going, we would stand at parade rest. Parade rest was different from attention, in that attention had your feet together and your arms at your side, your fingers curled into a loose fist with thumb at the seam of your trousers, eyes straight ahead, absolutely no looking anywhere other than straight ahead at the back of the head of the airman in front of you. Parade rest required your feet to be shoulder-width apart, back stiff and straight, arms behind your back with hands at the small of your back, and fingers extended.

Airman Second Class Whitson would patrol through the ranks so quietly that you wouldn't even know he was behind you. If, after a few hours, you unconsciously relaxed your fingers and they curled a bit, Airman Second Class Whitson would hit the ends of your fingers with the pith helmet he wore. The pain would shoot clear up to the base of your skull.

In case you haven't caught on by now, other than "sir," "Airman Second Class Whitson" was the only way we were allowed to address Airman Second Class Whitson.

So we could more easily understand our station in life and the vocation we'd pursue for the next four years, we got free haircuts. We stood at a door in the rear of a building and went in one at a time. The airman in front of me was seated when I went in. He was telling the haircut airman how he liked his hair cut. He was told, "Sure, I can do that," just before the electric clippers went from the base of his skull to the crown of his forehead, taking all the hair with it. We all received the same style of haircut: one-eighth-inch long all over. No one's hat fit after that. They all sat on our ears. Together with one-piece fatigues that were a couple of sizes too large we were, once again, informed of our status by our appearance.

In order to place each airman into the kind of work that would benefit the air force most, they gave you a battery of tests to determine your most innate skill set. Then you went to school to learn that trade/skill. This was called your Air Force Specialty Code (AFSC). Mine was 11314667. I'll never forget it. Surprisingly one test demonstrated that I was proficient with mechanics.

One of the other aptitude tests we had to take was a listening test, where the sound of beeps and boops where played through earphones and we were to write the letter the sounds stood for. It started slowly, like *Beep beep boop boop beep*, and ended sounding like *Beepboopboopboopbeep*. It was a test of Morris code. I had an aptitude for this, so I was assigned to airborne radio operator school. I was going to fly!

I had finished my basic six weeks' training and was at the desk of the airman who would process me out of Lackland Air Force Base and on to the next base in Biloxi, Mississippi, where I was to be trained. The orders were on the desk and signed. The airman was about to hand them to me when his phone rang. He answered, and then took out his red pen—the infamous red pen. He red-lined "Airborne Radio Operator" and wrote in "Air Craft Maintenance." That's how I ended up at Sheppard Air Force Base in Wichita Falls, Texas, learning aircraft maintenance with

Air Force Specialty Code (AFSC) 11314667: The air force didn't have enough students in that training class.

*What's best for the organization you're in isn't always what's best for you.*

The day before I mustered out of Lackland, there had been a party in our barracks. It took place after our duffel bags were in the bus and we were about to leave. It was a very private party. It was a blanket party, and the guest of honor was Airman Second Class Whitson.

I got settled into my routine of classes and continuation of basic military training at Sheppard Air Force Base. The base wasn't much different than Lackland, but we did have a pool and more time off. Over the next four months, I was taught the principles of electricity, pneumatics, hydraulics, and internal combustion engines. I was also given a security clearance level of secret.

Graduation day from Sheppard AFB was a big deal. We learned where our permanent base would be. I got Lockbourne AFB in Columbus, Ohio, and I was going to be in the Strategic Air Command (SAC). The very thing the movie named *Strategic Air Command*, starring Jimmy Stewart, was about and had enticed me into the air force.

# SAC

∞

When I checked in at Lockbourne AFB, my wing was on temporary duty (TDY) in Rabat, North Africa. The air force is divided into groups by command—Wing—Squadron. TDY was something I learned to live with. Each airman had an AWOL bag with clothes and personal supplies enough for four days. There were practice drills held without notice and at various times, where we'd grab our AWOL bags and beat it down to the hangar on the flight line. The "alerts" were different each time. Sometimes we'd mill around for a few hours; then the alert would be ended and we'd go back to the barracks. Other times, we'd get the planes that were in periodic dock (that's when a plane would be in for regular inspection and overhaul after 200 flying hours) put back together and pushed out of the hangar and onto the tarmac, ready for takeoff. Then there were times when all the planes of the wing were gotten off the ground. One of those alerts could last a few hours, with us flying around, before it was called off. One time, we flew up to our forward base in Goose Bay, Newfoundland, and stayed there three days.

I had a new roommate check in, and he was different from my other roommates. He was a staff sergeant, and they usually stayed in the non-com barracks. He was about the raunchiest airman I'd ever seen. We all kept up a good military appearance, though not as severe as it had been in basic training. Not him. There were days when he didn't even shave. He was a lifer and had been in since the air force was the Army Air Corps. He'd been a master sergeant a couple of times and busted from that rank a couple of times. He'd talk about his experiences in WWII and Korea a bit, but not much. He was an APG guy too: that's airplane general specialist.

One day, we were told there were going to be some big-deal generals visiting our base, and there was to be a parade in their honor. We were told to dress in our class A uniforms, with all the medals and ribbons. The first sergeant looked at my roommate and said we were to wear the medals, not just the ribbons that represented them. Next morning, we got into our dress uniforms and headed for the flight line. There was a gate we had to pass through to get to the hangar where we were to form up. There was usually an APE, as we called them—actually AP (air police)—on guard there.

This day, there were a couple of officers there, which was really unusual. The custom, requirement really, was for the enlisted personnel to initiate a salute, then for the officer to return the salute. I prepared to salute as we got closer to the gate, but both officers beat me, us, to it and snapped to with a stiff salute, so we ended up returning their salute. When we got closer to the hangar, our first sergeant did the same thing. I asked my roommate what the hell was going on, and that was when I noticed the light blue ribbon around his neck with the little white stars on it. The Congressional Medal of Honor was hanging around his neck. He was taken to the front of the formation. When we were back at our room, I asked him about that, and all I got was, "Yeah, I've had it for a while now." Then he told me he was close to retirement and was there to serve out the last few months he had to do.

*Some people really do not like attention they don't feel they deserve.*

Payday was every two weeks: $56. That weekend, we partied. The next weekend, everyone was broke, so it was card games in the barracks. I'd learned while playing seven and a half in our coal shed back in Gibbstown that it was the bank, dealer, in blackjack that made the money. Problem for me was you had to have enough money to be the bank, and I didn't have any.

Having money on the off weekend proved advantageous. You could lend it out for outrageous interest. Lend $20 and get $25. And those airmen were thrilled to pay it: Amazing.

I stayed in a few weekends and built up a bank. I started making money from blackjack from there on.

Came a day when someone was overdue with paying back. I'd been hanging around for a while with a guy from California, and he went with me to see the guy who owed me the money. He wasn't in his room, but his roommate was. Came to find out the guy was in a card game down the hall. I sent his roommate to get him. The guy came back and cried poor mouth—he didn't have it. Go get it from somebody in the game. Off he went, a little shaky, and came back with it. He had one of those balsa wood model planes he was building, the kind with all the skinny sticks parts. I broke it and put it on his bunk. He said I didn't have to do that when he gave me what he owed.

*Shaky people will do things you want them to do.*

I had a new roommate show up. He'd re-upped for four more years. He was from Pittsburgh. Why on earth would a guy re-up into this mess? I never really got a good answer to that question, but I think it was the signing bonus. The first weekend he was around, he asked if I knew where he could borrow a car. I didn't, but he found one. He asked me to show him around Columbus. Sure thing. It was an off weekend, and I was broke from lending my money out. We went to a couple of places before he was content being where we were. It was the bartender, us, and four other people in there. My roommate was a boisterous type. "Give me and my friend another drink, and get one for everybody else." He tossed a $20 onto the counter and got into conversation with the other people at the bar. He repeated his "Get one for everyone" thing and dropped another $20. He handed me a bunch of crumpled bills and whispered to me, "Take this and get me a couple of $20 from some place." I said okay and ran off to the closest bar and got two $20s. I did that one more time before we left, impressed with my new roommate's free spending. Turned out he didn't spend all that much, but the bartender and other people remembered him breaking $20 after $20.

He asked about the base cleaners and took some clothes there. That was nothing really out of line, but he seemed really interested in off-base housing, base pricing for cleaning, and how many airmen were in our wing's barracks. Over the next couple of weeks, he went looking for someone who had a panel truck he could use, and found one. He dug through the phone book for something called a bulk plant, and then off we went to visit a couple of them. He got a few big white canvas bags, and back at the barracks, he started visiting all the rooms and talking to airmen. He would pick up cleaning from some airmen and take it to the bulk plant and then bring it back. He became a clothes cleaning service. Pickup and drop-off at the same price as the base cleaners. By the time I got out of the air force, he owned four trucks outright and had people working for him. He was pulling in the cash.

*Find a need you can fill and charge for it.*

Early into getting his business off the ground, there was an off weekend, and we were about broke. I was ready for Saturday in the barracks, but not him. Back to the same bar we'd first gone to. Between us, we had $10, a boisterous guy, and a "Buy a drink for everybody" attitude. We were broke. It didn't matter. The people in the place all remembered him, and we drank that afternoon on the other people.

I learned what seed money is.

Most of the airmen, at least those in my part of the air force, were from Appalachia and the Confederate States, where there apparently was limited opportunity for "the good life." The Civil War was still being fought in the minds of many of them. Some of us were interested in the thinking of the people on the other side and didn't share the rancor that seemed to permeate many conversations. That being the case, Les invited me to go to his hometown in Clarksburg, West Virginia. The real instigation for this trip came from an airman from Turkey Creek, Kentucky.

Mail call produced a small package for this airman, can't remember his name, and it was a small bottle of cough syrup, or so I thought. Keep in mind I was not a worldly person. It was "shine" from home. I had no idea what shine was, which became a case for me being the butt of verbal jabs. Once I was educated, I wanted a taste. No way. *No way*, I was informed. There wasn't very much to start with, and he was not about to give any away.

I need to tell you a little about this fella from Turkey Creek: He would never be accused of being a handsome guy—quite the opposite. He had a sort of Popeye eye and a cheek deformed from having a chaw in it since he was a small child. He came to my attention while we were standing outside waiting for our haircut. When Airman First Class Whitson announced "Smoke 'em if you got 'em," just about every one of us pulled out a pack of cigarettes and proceeded to light up. Being it had been more than a month since I'd had a cigarette, which the first deep drag affected me so strongly I knelt down to keep from falling down. I was not alone.

Our boy from Turkey Creek didn't smoke. He asked Airman Second Class Whitson if he could have a chaw, which caught my attention since I remembered good ole Jonas.

Airman Second Class Whitson, being who he was, barked, "I see any spit, and you'll be a sorry-ass airman." Our airman from Turkey Creek ate, slept, and marched with a chaw in his cheek from then on.

After a steady stream of entreaties from me, our airman from Turkey Creek finally allowed me to have one cap full of "shine." Not even a teaspoonful, and my eyes watered, my tongue went numb, and I couldn't catch my breath. God that was awful stuff.

So that was how we got to talking about moonshine. Les told me his grandfather had a still in Clarksburg and ran shine to market in hopped-up '40 Fords. I wanted to see this, and he wanted to show me so off to Clarksburg we went.

We drove on a twisting and turning blacktop road for a few miles, then traveled on a dirt rut road for a while, then parked at the edge of a tree line. We walked toward a mountain for some distance, but then Les stopped and told me we weren't going to go to the still. What? After all this and being this close? Les didn't know if his grandfather was there or who was there, but he was sure whoever it was wouldn't know who I was, and maybe not even who he was, which meant the reaction of whoever was there might be to shoot us. "You're not serious?"

"There are people who drop out of sight around here, and nobody ever finds out where they went."

Les was not joking, or, from the look on his face, exaggerating. I didn't get to see a still, but I'm convinced it was there.

I did get to display some more of my ignorance though. I commented to Les that we customized our '40 Fords so they rode front high, not like the ones I saw around there which were rear high. He took me over to one that someone he knew owned, opened the trunk and showed me a large tank in there. "When this is full the car runs level."

Being a moonshiner was not something you just decide to be. You have to be from the area, and anyway, it's just too risky.

On my twenty-first birthday, my father gave me the best lesson in life I've ever gotten. I was celebrating my birthday at a party "downtown," as we called being off base, and we ran out of beer. I volunteered to go get more, so I borrowed a car and went off on my mission. The streets in that part of town allowed parking on both sides. The street was narrow. I rounded a corner too fast. My reactions weren't all that good, and the car I was driving had what was called bubble skirts over the wheel wells. I sideswiped a parked car with a skirt, and as I turned to see what that noise was, I crossed to the other side of the street and sideswiped another car, did the same thing again, and crashed square into the rear of another parked car. I climbed out of the car, leaned on the hood, and took in the litter down the whole block. Sirens and cops, a ride in a cop van, a blur of processing stuff, and standing in a dank hallway on the phone with my dad and a cop a few feet away.

"You were at a birthday party—your birthday party—and got into a car crash?"

"How old are you now?"

"I'm twenty-one."

"That's some mess. Call me and let me know how you make out." *Click.*

And I felt what it's like to be responsible for your actions.

During my military years, I'd learned things a fella could do with girls. I met one at a dance in Reynoldsburg, Ohio, that stood out from the rest. Her dad wasn't a fan of me. Her mom was neutral.

I served four years to the day and was released from active duty in February 1960. After I put in two additional years of reserve duty, I received an honorable discharge from the Armed Forces of the United States of America on February 15, 1962.

Here are some of the things for which I received official recognition:

- The United States Armed Forces Institute Certificate of Successful Completion of Tests of General Educational Development High School Level (December 1959)

- The State of New Jersey Department of Education High School Equivalency Certificate (April 1960)

- Department of the Air Force Outstanding Unit award

- United States Air Force Certificate of Proficiency Specializing in Aircraft Mechanic Reciprocating over Two Engines (August 21, 1956)

- Department of the Air Force Certificate of Training Camp

- Department of the Air Force 10-Hour Driver Improvement Course (May 1958)

- Dynamics of moral leadership physical fitness test (September 16, 1958)

- United States Armed Forces Institute test, General Education Development,

- High School Level (December 1959)

- Progress individual ground training record baseline security pays to security phase 3 security and qualification APCs survival.

- Good Conduct medal

- Training in small arms familiarization

# The 1960s

# HOME AGAIN

I returned home to Gibbstown on leave for a couple of weeks before being discharges and went looking for my neighborhood friends. I walked into Billy Burt's, and there at the bar was Johnny. He was the kid who would beat me up just to have something to do before I went into the air force. He greeted me with "Hi, Sonny" (my nickname) and a punch on my arm, which was the regular way guys would greet each other—only, Johnny's punch was hard enough to really hurt. Now, Johnny had a sadistic streak in him and would punch his grandmother while she was sitting in her rocking chair, for no reason. The whole neighborhood was intimidated by him. I returned his greeting with a punch on his arm that took him clear off his barstool and down on the floor.

Sonny was gone, and George had arrived.

Back in Gibbstown, I started looking for a job. Since I was trained and had worked at it for four years, I applied with several airlines for work as an aircraft mechanic.

My training and experience qualified me to attend an airlines school for mechanics, and then maybe a job. After graduating from school, I would be placed in a maintenance job someplace where the airline needed a mechanic. I'd just spent four years in Texas; Columbus, Ohio; Goose Bay, Newfoundland; Thule, Greenland; the Azores; and Rabat, North Africa. I wanted to stay in New Jersey.

So much for military training.

My dad and my mom had divorced while I was in the air force, and I wasn't aware of it. He lived with his new wife, and Mom had a boyfriend named Pete. Pete had been in the Vietnam thing and suffered from the effects of Agent Orange. He worked at the New York Ship Yards, which was in on the Delaware River in Camden, New Jersey. My secret clearance and Pete's connection got me a job at the shipyard as a machinist helper setting machines in the NS *Savannah*, the first nuclear freighter/passenger ship. I worked in the CV (containment vessel) of the nuclear engine. I learned of India blue ink and grinding mounting plates so it was perfectly flat to set a machine.

Safety wasn't such a big deal in the shipyard. There was an overhead crane they used to move huge steel plates from one end of the ship to the other. Some guy would wrap a sling around an eight-foot-by-sixteen-foot, half-inch plate that was lying on the deck and throw the loop onto a hook. The crane operator would run the crane to the other end of the deck, with the plate swinging wildly right above the heads of everyone on the deck. I worked below decks in compartments helping set machines. The machine was swung into the compartment from a hook welded to the ceiling. Someone was welding a hook on the ceiling of the compartment below us, and I watched the red-hot line moving across the floor right toward where we were sitting on the deck. If I hadn't seen it coming, we would have been seriously burned.

Quitting time was an adventure. We'd clean up our work area and take the tools back to the shop, then wait at the shop door for the quitting-time whistle. When it sounded, we headed for the gates, which were nearly fifty yards away. Our time cards were in a rack on the Yard side of a turnstile. We grabbed our time card, pushed through the turnstile, slid the card into the time clock to have it punched, put the card in the slot on the street side of the turnstile, and headed for the parking lot across the street. There had to be twenty turnstiles. There were thousands of people working at the shipyard, and they all were dashing to get out of there at the same time.

Once, there was a big fuss halfway between the shops and the turnstiles. Some guy was stealing copper tubing by winding it around his chest and hiding it under his shirt. The exertions of getting out made him breathe heavily. The tubing restricted his chest movement, and he collapsed to the ground.

On the other side of the turnstiles, there was the sidewalk and then the street that ran in front of the shipyard, then the parking lot. The crush of people heading for the parking lot crowded into the street all along the two blocks like a wave, blocking cars trying to drive by. There were traffic lights along the two blocks of turnstiles, but they didn't make much difference. When the lights turned red, what little movement the cars made came to a halt. I saw one guy open the back door of a car and then climb through and go out the other door. The local people knew to avoid the shipyard at quitting time.

Such was the life of a shipyard worker. Not for me.

I went to my dad to see if he could get me a job at the mill. I started working for DuPont at the entry (laborer) level. This was mowing grass, picking up trash, and cleaning floors—that kind of thing. When a person was needed in one of the operations (where products were actually made), they'd send a request to the labor department, and the person who had been there longest was sent to the operation.

*There is something to be said for nepotism.*

By the time I got around to working at the Repauno Plant, it had changed a good deal. The dynamite and black powder operations had been moved elsewhere and were replaced with other nasties that would explode. The main product became DMT (dimethyl terephthalate acid). This is the stuff Dacron is made from. DMT was made in huge metal tanks called oxidizers, where the chemical reaction took place. They sometimes took off like rockets and were housed in thick-walled metal cells. There were many other operations too. One of them was NH3 (anhydrous ammonia).

While in the labor pool, four of us were sent to the equipment shed. It was a very warm day. We were given several large sets of ice tongs and some very large crowbars. We put our tools onto a wagon and went out to the magazines on Magazine Lake. Our task was to pull up old railroad ties. These ties had been in place since before the war—that's WWII—and they had grown into part of the terrain. Pulling them out was a difficult physical task, and hot work. We used crowbars to work the ties loose and then used the tongs to pull them out and put them on the flat wagon. This kind of work reminded me of the guys I watched when I was a child. After we had several rows stacked on the wagon, we rode the wagon to various locations around the plant and offloaded them into small open spaces. This task took a number of weeks, and the reason for that was that we were not in the physical condition it took to do the work, and we needed the time to build up to the task. Finally, there were enough ties spread around that we were finished, or so we thought. Talk about a crash physical fitness program! And I thought the military had been rough!

Bright and early on a Monday morning, we were told to report to the equipment shed again. We thought we were done with railroad ties, and we were. The part of getting the ties out was done, but building the parking lots with them was not. We were detailed to build parking lots using the old railroad ties as parking stops. We were issued sixteen-pound sledgehammers and a stack of one-inch pipes cut to twenty-four-inch length. Railroad ties were all placed where they needed to be, and we were to drive in four pipes to hold each in place. We didn't consider driving a one-inch pipe into regular ground to be a big deal, but surprise, this wasn't regular ground. There had been red brick buildings where there now was going to be parking lots.

DuPont was very safety conscious, for obvious reasons, so there were standard rules for safety equipment. Among them was to always wear gloves and steel-toed shoes and safety glasses and a hard hat. Now, consider swinging a sixteen-pound sledgehammer overhead, aiming at a one-inch target, with all that in the way. The gloves were high-quality leather. That meant in order to hold the hammer so it wouldn't slip from your grip on the way down, you had to squeeze very hard. Something else we learned: swinging a hammer tended to pull you forward as it swung, and pulling you forward threw your aim off so the head of the hammer went beyond the top of the pipe. This resulted in the handle of the hammer coming down on the pipe. With this came a horrific vibration and shock that coursed through your whole upper body as well as broke handles, which needed to be replaced. For the first few weeks, we went through hammer handles faster than they could be purchased. More physical fitness training!

We got to the point where we could control our hammers and stopped breaking handles. One day, while eating with operations people, one of them commented about the size of the guns (arms) on us. We'd not noticed since we'd been together all along. Then came the day when one of us was promoted and a new guy joined the crew. No one thought to warn the poor guy. On the first swing he made, he overcompensated for the pull of the hammer, and the edge of the head just clipped the top of the pipe, and then continued its arch until it hit his shin. The hollow sound—*thock*—as the hammer drove his leg out from under him backward almost turned our stomachs. We all instantly appreciated how we'd grown from the work we were doing.

I had been bow-and-arrow shooting since I was a teenager and had been using a sixty-pound, recurve fiberglass bow with no stack. A stacked bow is one which becomes more difficult to pull as you draw it. The full stored power of the bow was reached when the arrow was fully drawn. The arrows were twenty-six inches long. My shoulders and arms had been toned from hunting and archery. I belonged to an indoor archery team. I hunted small game and ducks with my bow and arrow. Flu-flu arrows had large spirally fletched feathers on them and slowed the arrow down so dramatically that they would only fly a short distance. My bow would shoot a regular arrow over one hundred yards, but a flu-flu only went about thirty. In distance, that was plenty far to lose the arrow, so you only got one shot per arrow, unless you could be positioned enough to shoot nearly straight up. A result of hunting with bow and arrow was that one Thanksgiving, our meal was composed of pheasant, duck, rabbit, and squirrel.

Of course, boys being boys, we got into arm wrestling contests. No one outside of our little parking lot gang could take any of us—except this one guy. He was an engineer. Ralph was his name. I took him on, and here's what happened: We started and it was a dead lock—at first. I couldn't push him over, and he couldn't move me. It was stalemate, sort of. When you're in one of these things, there is a second-wind kind of thing that happens. I went first with my super effort. Ralph didn't budge. Ralph took his shot, and my arm position didn't move either. My arm stayed locked, but Ralph rotated my whole locked body so my butt lifted off the chair and I was lying sideways. In line, but sideways. Now that was impressive. I'm right-handed, but I sometimes wrestled left. On one occasion, something in my arm let loose, I don't know what; but I have this little knot on the outside of my forearm where whatever let loose is. I've felt no consequence other than a realization and a permanent memento from the experience.

*Be very aware of potential consequences of physical strength tests.*

The fashion of the day was Edwardian-cut jackets and bell-bottom trousers, which was perfect for me. I had a thirty-two-inch waist and wore a 44 jacket. My biceps and forearms were at 15 inches. T-shirts were a tight fit at the arms.

After a while in the labor pool, I was brought into the ammonia operation at the lowest job classification: helper. I took readings in the field and samples over to the lab. There were different levels of pay grade. Each had an outline of duties. It was shift work. I had a problem adjusting to night work, but I did it because that was the job. What with heat exchangers, cracking towers, high-pressure gaseous and liquid flows and chemical reactions, I found the workings of a continuous chemical manufacturing operation very interesting. I had a strong curiosity for how and why things did what they did.

The control room showed the whole operation in diagram, from methane through all the steps to becoming ammonia. There were levels of operator and promotions based upon longevity and knowledge. I applied myself and studied the diagrams and operation manuals until I understood the whole place. I got *how* it all worked, if not *why*.

# JOBS AND LAYOFFS

There were periods of slack business, and people were laid off during those times. Layoffs were done by seniority, and recalls were done in reverse seniority. I got caught up in one of those. The rumor was that this could be a long layoff, so I began collecting unemployment money and started looking for work.

I applied at the Hercules plant in Gibbstown, Del Monte in Swedesboro, and Cardox in Gibbstown, as well as searched through the newspaper.

There was nothing happening, but after a couple of weeks, I got a call from a newspaper ad I'd answered. It was selling encyclopedias and was based in Philly.

I went to check it out and was hired for door-to-door sales. We were taught schemes for gaining entrance into homes and the pitch to use to talk people into buying a set. Each day, six days a week, we were taken to a section of the city and dropped off on a corner, told the boundary of the area we were to cover, and the time and place to be picked up.

There was this one day when I learned something about this kind of sales. I was looking at a huge apartment building that I was to cover. Off I went: Knock, knock. "Hello, I'm from—" Slam. Then: Knock, knock. "Hello—" Slam. And so it went until I got to thinking about what I was doing. There is someone in this big building who wants a set of encyclopedia, and all I have to do is find them. I junked the entrance pitch idea and set off to find the one who wanted what I was selling.

Knock, knock. "I'm selling the best encyclopedia there is—you interested?"

"No." Slam.

This went on for a while. Then, knock, knock: "I'm selling the best encyclopedia there is—you interested?"

"Honey, there's somebody here selling encyclopedias, you know how we were just talking about that? Come in, let's see what you have." I sold three sets that night. The whole crew of five of us might sell that many in a night.

Then on another day, I had my greatest sales feat of anything, anywhere. We were dropped off in a trailer park on Saturday afternoon. As I worked my way along a street, I came to some guy painting the little fence by his trailer. He was too busy to listen to me. I volunteered to help him paint his fence so we could talk about what I was selling. He said he was a Seventh-day Adventist and couldn't be seen talking to me. We finished the fence and went into the trailer. The first thing I noticed was a set of encyclopedias.

He told me again that he was a Seventh-day Adventist and he couldn't talk business. I didn't know what that meant. My Catholic training did not include what he said. I sold him a set. Their second set at that!

I was given a different business opportunity by one of the other people in my encyclopedia group. The guy told me he had a way to win at a horse racetrack. He had a system and needed a partner. Sure, you have a system. If it was so good, why was he selling encyclopedias? It was his partner's fault, he said. He explained the system to me, and I told him I'd think about it but had no intention of doing that. Back in Gibbstown, at the barber shop, which was the center for all such things, I asked Nick the barber about this system. He said there were some schemes that did work, but you had to stick to the scheme, and most people didn't because they didn't pay very much money. Since then, I've had a few occasions to use this scheme, and it does work. If you want to win a lot, you have to bet very large amounts and have a large reserve bankroll. Statistics of horse racing show that the second post favored horse will run in the money 75 percent of the time. At post time, you bet on the second post favored horse to show. If the horse runs out, on the next race, you double your bet. If that horse runs out, you double your bet again. If that horse runs out, you go back to the original bet. Averages being what they are, there will be times when your horse will pay in streaks and lose in streaks. You must think in business terms, not gambling terms, and have enough reserve money to ride out the losing streak. You must resist the urge to go out of your system when a big winning streak hits or dip into your reserve for anything other than betting.

I left my encyclopedia job and was offered a job by the Hercules Powder Company. This company was a spinoff from DuPont. DuPont had been found to be monopolizing the explosives business, so they created a separate company, Hercules Powder Company, so they were no longer monopolizing it. Hercules headquarters was in the DuPont building in Wilmington. The international headquarters of DuPont and their plant in Gibbstown abutted the DuPont plant there. They made something called para-cresol. My job was to take large containers of waste back into the marsh, by the river, and dump it. This was some really foul-smelling stuff. The odor soaked into your clothes. I didn't like smelling like that.

I was next hired by the Cardox Corporation. Their plant made dry ice from $CO_2$. They got their $CO_2$ from the waste $CO_2$ discharged from the $NH_3$ plant in DuPont. The two plants were connected by an underground 24-inch pipe a half-mile long. The $CO_2$ gas was compressed and, under pressure, turns into liquid form for ease of storage.

I was brought in as an ice press operator. The liquid $CO_2$ was released into a press at atmospheric pressure, where it turned into snow and was squeezed into a block of ice. I ran the presses and band saws that cut the big blocks into smaller blocks of sixty pounds and then loaded 1,012 of them into a refrigerated train car.

The recall to DuPont came, and back I went.

*There is something to be said for the longevity system of filling demands for workers.*

## Instrumentation

DuPont trained their tradesmen: electricians, instrumentation, lagging, pipe fitting, machinists, millwrights, and the like took apprentice training courses. The mechanics got the highest pay among wage roll people. I wanted the most money, I could get, so I went after an apprenticeship.

Every so many years, a class opened for apprenticeships and there was a testing session for anyone who wanted to become a skilled laborer. The bidding for skills apprenticeships began with the person with the highest grade on the test getting first choice. Instrumentation was the elite skill and most sought after.

*Experience and knowledge are good things.*

I got to be an instrumentation apprentice and experienced holding the lowest paying position on the plant. I was making less than when I was in the Labor pool but the opportunity for promotion and pay raises was far greater and worth the sacrifice.

One day a week we were in a classroom where an instructor guided us through all the different disciplines our chosen skill required. Being in instrumentation I got to take the most courses. The courses were through the International Correspondence Schools and included: English, math, algebra, hydraulics, pneumatics, mechanical drawing, electricity, and electronics. The rest of the time we worked with 1st class mechanics. I completed my Instrument Apprenticeship course work in January of 1965 and my apprenticeship in October of 1965.

*Documentation of education is important.*

My incentive to be a good provider for my family wasn't a conscious idea. It was just something I needed to do. It showed itself on the day we woke up to snow being over two feet deep. We lived in an apartment between Ashton's Bend and the crossroads where Gibbstown turned into Paulsboro, about three miles from the C-line gate. My car, a 1954 Ford flathead V8, wouldn't start. I walked to work. The wind was blowing so that the snow was coming down sideways. It was bitterly cold. I caught a ride by Billy Burt's quarter mile from the C-line gate.

I was looking to make as much money as I could and my career path had that potential with five steps of progression. It went from apprentice to bottom of second class mechanic to top of second to bottom of first to top of first. I received a Certificate of Completion Instrument

Apprenticeship and was promoted to bottom of second class instrument mechanic.

I applied myself and in April of 1967, I received a certificate of award for suggesting a change to Xylol flow control, which greatly improved the efficiency of the operation. I made it to top of first without incident.

> *Distinguishing yourself from the pack can be a good thing.*

There came a day when my wife and her friend were going shopping. She came in to get my help because she'd gotten the car stuck in the mud of the driveway. She managed to get the car rotated so the front end was angled toward one of the sycamore trees that lined the drive. The car was just close enough to the tree that I could put my feet against it while grabbing the bumper with both hands and lie on the hood of the car. I told her to try to slowly back away while I pushed. You know how there is a slack range where a car can be raised before the full weight is taken up? I remember the look they had on their faces as I strained against the car. It lifted until I was looking down at them, giving the impression I'd lifted the car off the ground. I came close, but not really. Both were wide-eyed as the car backed out of the drive.

We had a softball team in the instrument shop, as did the other shops and operations around the plant. We were still, figuratively, working on our pecking order, and there were foot races before the softball games. I volunteered to be the official starter of one of the races. I started them off, ran on ahead, and declared the winner. I could run.

Darts season ended right around the time softball season started. I joined a couple of softball teams outside of the plant. My name appeared in the newspaper about every week for outstanding play of some sort. Each year, I looked for a league with better talent, as I did with Darts. There was a countywide league, and I wanted to play on it, so I went to an early practice to try out. I knew a few of the guys on the field, so I joined them for fungo practice. That's where someone hits fly balls into the outfield. There was banter and a relaxed, loose atmosphere as the balls were hit and caught. I noticed that after a ball was caught, it was nonchalantly thrown back—in the air. We were pretty far out in the field for this kind of thing. I could throw a soft ball a hundred yards, but even? Once in a while, someone would catch a high fly behind his back. These were teams that had been in play for a number of years, and the talent level was greater than I'd known at that point. There were players there who had been in the big leagues—they were that good. I quickly understood that a position in the outfield was not available, so the position I had been playing, third base, was where I needed to try to play. There was, of course, someone already at that position, so I'd have to win it. Then came time for infield workout, and I was asked where I wanted to play. Third, I said.

The general attitude of about everyone was, *That position is taken*, but I was given permission to take few balls at third. It was time to show off. In one smooth motion, I let the ball slide into my glove and then sent it on its way to first, returned to third base bag and waited for the ball to return to me after going around the horn. The captain was the one hitting the practice balls, and each time around the field, he picked up the pace. It got to where the balls were coming at a clip good enough to pop my glove. This meant everything picked up, including the 'round-the-horn pace. As an alert that it was shifting into high gear, "We ready?" came from the captain. He smoked one at me; I picked it off with no problem and fired it to first. The guy over there wasn't the regular first baseman, and my ball took his glove off his hand. He picked it up and announced, "I'm not standing here for this stuff." I'd passed my test for third base. Next came hitting. I'm right-handed and could put the ball on the right field baseline almost at will. I passed the hitting test and won a chance to play on the team. I also shared third base and shortstop.

In a game, when I was at shortstop, a hit ball bounced high over the third baseman's head, and I picked it off deep in the hole. As I planted my foot to fire it to first, I was looking down at my planted foot when I saw my leg go into an L-shape. The knee had popped under the strain.

That was the end of my softball career.

I was an umpire for a few seasons and found that to be satisfying. I told the captains before each game that I

113

understood the emotion of their players and would tolerate some expression of disagreement. If someone jumps in the air while criticizing a call, I'll let it go, unless they come back down. In that case, I'll throw them out of the game. Everyone caught on. I had no problems.

There is one memory: It was a call at second base when a player was stretching a hit into a double, and I called him out. I was behind the plate calling the game. Many times, we only had two umpires; and the plate ump had home, third, and, in some situations, second. One player thought he was safe and came up ready to argue. That was when he saw we were face-to-face. I'd been right on top of the play.

*Amateur softball umpiring doesn't pay enough to be a vocation.*

# CHEMICAL INDUSTRIAL UNION (CIU)

∞

Promotion required a person to demonstrate the ability to perform the work and possess the knowledge required by the next level. After a set amount of time at each level, without negative notations in your record, you were automatically given the promotion to the next level and the raise that went with it. There was no minimum time between top of second class to bottom of first class, and I asked about that from my foreman and supervisor and union rep, but I didn't get a satisfactory answer. Management could hold a person at second class indefinitely.

We had a union, but it was what is termed a company union. Read: powerless.

I got a copy of the Work Agreement between the Chemical Industrial Union (CIU) and DuPont and read through it. There were specific things and lengths of time in class required to move from apprentice to second class and to top of second and from bottom of first to top of first, but nothing about moving from top of second to bottom of first. My interest in the CIU began. I attended union meetings and learned the answer to my question had to come from the "company," and the question could only be asked by someone on the union board of directors.

How does a person get on the BOD, was my next question. You have to be elected.

I learned about progression within the CIU.

Shop Steward was the first step, so I ran for that against a fellow instrument mechanic and won by one vote. The guy I ran against was a nice-enough fellow. We played on the shop softball team and played darts together. Being the sportsman he was, he'd voted for me in the election and was surprised I didn't vote for him!

The next step was to be elected to the Board of Directors. There were only five positions, and these were positions of prestige, which meant they were sought after by more than a few. I looked over the positions available and saw one wasn't as sought after: Recording Secretary. No one wanted to take minutes and record them. I wanted to be on the Board. I did some self-teaching and, after a fashion, learned to type. Because I was an instrument mechanic, I got around the whole plant and could campaign everywhere. I was elected to the BOD. Being the Recording Secretary was easy. Next, it was to be appointed to the contract negotiating committee. Since the majority of people on the BOD were afraid to upset the apple cart and speak up, getting on the negotiating committee was a snap.

I learned that wanting something is the first important step. Then look for the best way to get to where you want to go, what it takes to do that, and then do it.

*Doing it is the difference between the big-talking, ne'er-do-well dreamers and achievers.*

I did a number of things that caught the attention of the Front Office. One of them had to do with there being no minimum time between 2nd class and 1st class. The people on the Contract Negotiating team with me were not aggressive. In fact, they were all but useless for trying to get things improved for members. I did some talking to our union lawyer and some research on the Landrum-Griffin and Taft-Hartley acts.

We had a bright young 2nd class mechanic in the shop that everyone liked and was thought of highly by management. I cooked up a scheme with Walt, which he didn't like very much. He was due for top of 2nd shortly.

The day after Walt was promoted to the top of 2nd, he and I went into the Foreman's office, and I asked that he be promoted to 1st class. At first, the Foreman, Baker; (Bake we called him), thought I was joking; but I convinced him I wasn't. I showed him the work agreement and where Walt didn't have to wait for any amount of time before he could be promoted. I asked what work Walt had been doing for the previous year, then proceeded to point out that Walt had been doing 1st class–level work and doing it on his own. This qualified him to be paid as 1st class mechanic.

We had a grievance procedure for addressing disagreements over contract language, and this went into those steps. My position permitted me to file a first-stage grievance and take that to a second-stage level, which was with the people we were negotiating with for the contract. It required a majority vote of the board to initiate a third stage. That's where the lawyer got involved and we started paying money. There were two on the board who would vote with the President, and he hadn't taken anything to arbitration since he became President. I think he was jockeying for a Foreman's job. That was the way Management took good union people out of Management's hair. They made them a member of Management.

I maintained that since Management could not show any reason for not promoting Walt, they must not be promoting him for personal reasons, in violation of a condition of the Agreement. In order to show that he didn't know enough to be promoted, they had to show what he had to know. That would be something Management avoided intensely: a job description.

Our union lawyer was convinced that we could get wording in the Agreement that would be a job description through pressing this grievance to arbitration. We had no power to force Management off any position they chose to take, except arbitration. We were in contract negotiations at the time. We had a strong position to put before an arbiter. This situation was felt all the way to Wilmington, and the highest level of Management because of the corporation-wide potential for job descriptions.

The President and others on the committee were for the negotiation path. Negotiations carried on from a couple of weeks before the contract expiration until the new contract was signed. Management, *in an effort to protect the workers*, agreed to abide by the terms of the old contract until the new one was accepted. In essence, we had a contract in perpetuity. We would win every argument but loose every battle. We didn't take this grievance to arbitration but chose to wait for the right time to bring it up in contract negotiations and have this as the weapon to force Management to provide job descriptions or a time period between top of 2nd and bottom of 1st. All this was going to take was enough sand in the craw of the other members of the BOD.

My strongest bit of understanding of power came in the form of what political power means to wage roll people. Each year, the DMT operation was shut down for overhaul and repair. There was lots of overtime available. Two older guys came to me during one of those shutdowns, with the complaint that they were being told they had to work a double shift after they'd already worked two doubles in a row. These guys were in their late fifties. My complaint, which also turned into a grievance, was that this was an unreasonable demand and placed the safety of the men and others in jeopardy. This grievance went all the way to arbitration. We won! It was the only arbitration the CIU had ever even taken to arbitration, let alone won. The Arbiter ruled the Company had a right to require a reasonable amount of overtime, and this went beyond that condition.

The next year, we had the same situation and the same exact complaint, but from two other guys. It was back to arbitration. This time we lost. What? The difference was the Arbiter ruled the company had a right to require workers to work overtime. He dropped one word: *reasonable*.

Dick Nixon was President during these arbitrations. Here's what I learned from this experience: Nixon wanted to do away with the National Labor Relations Board, or at least the American Arbitration Association (AAA.) He and his people did not like the way the AAA was ruling in arbitrations in general. They were slanted in the workers' favor. Since this would have eliminated government support for the working class in such an obvious way, it might have brought on strong reaction against the Republican Party. Cooler heads worked their magic, and instead of eliminating the AAA, the members were replaced with pro-corporation lawyers.

*The value of combined voices of workers in the area of safety, working conditions, and pay can be trumped by*

*politics; and people can be induced to vote against their*
*own best interest.*

Over the next five years, I began digging into a few other things at the Plant where I worked. One of which was the Pension Plan. I wanted to know the formula for deciding how much money was put into the Pension Trust Fund. The money in the fund was defined as belonging to the people of DuPont and clearly stated the Company could gain no benefit in interest or principle from it. None of this was in the Agreement but was in the Plan description and as such, became a part of the Agreement.

The Union President didn't want this to become a grievance, and I couldn't get around him, so I shut up. Phil, the union President, was getting aggravated with what I was doing. Sometime later, Phil went on sick leave for an operation of some type, and I got my chance. Within two weeks, I had a work action with lots of people walking a picket line in front of the plant. Strict rules for being on the line included no one could interfere with traffic going into or out of the plant, or production. Truck drivers, who were Teamsters, would not voluntarily violate the picket line. The Union lawyer saw what we were doing as a good negotiating tool. We had the attention of Management. Newspaper reporters were asking questions, and a negative image of DuPont was being shown. All we wanted was to provide a little incentive to the Management negotiators to get the contract negotiations over. We knew, of course, that meant the people in Wilmington had to be involved. It also meant the local people were being viewed as, maybe, not competent. All of Management had something to be concerned about, and that suited me just fine.

I'll digress for a moment. The DuPont Corporation was so sensitive to its image that they wouldn't even have the name on the side of trucks for fear that in the event of a traffic accident, people would see it. Remember, there were trucks filled with all manner of nasties.

Another thing I was interested in was pay raises. We were guaranteed by Federal law to be able to talk to decision makers during negotiations, and we were told over and over again that those Management people at the table were decision makers. I decided to take that on. When wage increases were the topic would be my time.

Once a year, Management would announce pay raises company wide, and everyone knew that came down from the head office in Wilmington, Delaware, where the real decision makers were. This year, the offer was 3 percent across the board. We were asking for 5 percent and going through the justification process we always went through. The management people did their best not to break into laughter and take what we were saying seriously.

This time was different. There were people picketing out front and newspaper reporters asking questions. At the right time, and with Phil out sick, I made my pitch to prove we were not talking to the management people empowered to make a decision: "We'll take 2 percent across the board, but you have to agree to that within the next two minutes, without leaving this room, or making or receiving any phone calls." There were flushed faces and pale faces and looks exchanged between the Management negotiators for the next, agonizing, two minutes. When I announced— Too Late—their faces were a reddish color. I'd gotten what I wanted—proof they were not negotiating in good faith. Something our lawyer told us would be our most powerful tool. They suggested we take a restroom break.

When we all got back, I changed the subject. Now let's talk about pensions: which of you is responsible for explaining how this is calculated? The specter of what had just happened with the pay increase was putting pressure on them. I laid the Pension Plan leaflet on the table.

They were looking around at each other. They feared the next few minutes were about to get even worse for them, and I intended to make them as bad as I could.

There was a knock on the door: it was the plant Superintendent's secretary. She whispered something to him, and he announced he had something that urgently had to be taken care of, so we needed to adjourn for the day. That knock on the door seemed a little too opportune for my taste.

Phil, the Union President, returned to work and put a halt to all of my initiatives posthaste. We never got back to negotiating with Management over the pension thing.

What is called an explosion is otherwise termed "rapid oxidation," which is something trying to burn very rapidly but held inside a container of some sort so the gaseous material being given off by the material when heated to a certain temperature can't expand the way it wants. When the pressure created gets greater than the container can hold, it fails, and we get what we call an explosion. When the explosive itself is left in the open and set on fire, it will just burn very quickly.

The burning grounds were on one end of the plant, and it was where leftover material from all manner of experiments were disposed of by open fire.

Rumor had it scientists were trying to mix liquid rocket fuel. Don't know for sure, but part of the experiment could be witnessed if a person knew where and when. I did. There were four small buildings (Labs) out by the burning grounds: three were lined along the riverbank and one was standing abreast of the middle of the three. This one was the control room. There was a boardwalk that connected all the labs.

I parked my truck across the road from the control room at the appropriate time. A small bell-shaped robot, about three feet tall, that moved on tracks like a small tank and had a camera mounted on the top, which gave the impression of being a head, appeared at the doorway and then came slowly out of the building on the left. It was holding a flask about a quarter full of liquid straight out in its one arm/hand. It wobbled along the uneven walkway to the next lab in line and entered. It stayed out of sight for five to ten minutes, and when it reappeared, the flask had more liquid in it. It wobbled on to the third lab and went in. It stayed out of sight for another ten minutes or so, and then—*whoosh!* An explosion jolted me, and a weak concussion hit the truck. This was accompanied by a huge cloud of very black smoke that blew from the top and out the doorway of the lab. Some minutes later, the little robot came out, blackened in streaks across the front, still holding the flask out straight, which had the bottom missing. The little thing wobbled back to the first lab and went in.

This was one of the places to get a chuckle during the workday.

This science stuff can be very interesting.

There were experiments being conducted all over the plant, for all manner of things. There was even one for making a boat using explosives by blowing aluminum plates into a mold.

The breadboard stage of testing comes after lab work has suggested a product may be created from a specific procedure for handling different chemicals.

The many experiments operated simultaneously, and I was assigned to assist with the one being done in this lab. I guessed this experiment was for creating liquid rocket fuel since the rumor mill had reported the Government hired DuPont to work on this project. This was one of several being conducted at the plant.

I was given a set of blueprints for setting up the controls for the experiment. All I needed to know was the parameters the temperatures, flows, levels, specific gravities, and acidity were to be maintained. What the materials were was of no consequence. On a Monday, I set up the processes in the small lab and tested everything. I had my work, which I completed by end of day Wednesday, checked off by the lab rat (what we called the Fuds [PhDs]) and went off to whichever other assignment I had.

The experiment was set up on Thursday and run on Friday. So far with the same results, as I saw it. Monday morning, I'd find tubing, instruments, and sensors all over the walls, floor, and ceiling. The thing had blown up—again. This wasn't a fire-breathing explosion; at least there weren't any charred remains.

And so the schedule continued: gather the pieces, parts that were salvageable, and calibrate that which needed to be calibrated. To new ranges, if there were any, obtain and install whichever replacement parts were needed and run alpha tests on the whole thing.

This working with the control mechanisms for continuous chemical production was very satisfying and challenging.

# FAMILY

The woman I met in Ohio, and I decided to get married and did so before the summer of 1961.

I needed a better job. Responsibility of a Dad.

You'll notice I refer to just myself throughout this book, and that's because the book is about selecting a blue-collar vocation without direction, which is what I did.

I got married in the Catholic Church in Woodbury, and, as was customary, we received counseling prior to our marriage. This counseling included being informed about the Catholic position on birth control. It was easy to understand: there was none permitted. But a couple could follow the timing of a woman's cycle of fertility and engage in sexual activity only during the times she was less fertile. We learned what people who practiced the rhythm cycle of birth control were called. Its parents.

Men who have no experience, by and large, write books and council people on sex? Give me a break!

Much later, the miracle called "The Pill" arrived. We were told that could only be used to regulate her cycle, not as a birth control device.

*Hypocrisy wasn't limited to people*

Things in nature taking their course, I soon became a father. Babies were foreign to me. I'd not even been in the same room with one. A few months following the blessed event, our child was crying in the middle of the night, and it was my turn to see to her needs. She had a clean diaper and didn't want her bottle, which exhausted my understanding of what to do when a baby cries. I'd walked around, rocking her in my arms for a while, but she kept crying. I sat down and had her on my lap, crying and gulping for breath between cries. My patience ran out—took her by the sides while I barked at her; "Shut up!"

She stopped crying, our eyes locked, and in that instant, I became a Dad. I'd frightened her and guilt flooded through me. I realized how dependent that innocent little person was on me for everything she needed. How helpless she was. I pulled her against my chest and rocked her gently, trying to undo what I'd just done. We both slept like that through the rest of the night.

*Being a Dad is, in a different way, more important than a full-time job.*

There was a blacksmith in the main shop of the plant where machinists and millwrights worked, and I was watching him work. There was a coke-fueled furnace with a cast iron pot hanging just clear of the white-hot coals. The blacksmith used a pair of tongs, picked up the pot of molten lead, and set the pot down on his open palm. He chuckled while I almost choked. He put the molten lead pot back on the coals. He let me stand there stunned a couple of minutes before he said anything. "The bottom of a pot is room temperature until the heat from whatever is in it soaks through."

When I got home that night, there was a pot of boiling water on the stove for pasta. I tried what the blacksmith had done and felt the bottom of the pot was actually room temperature, but I felt it heating up really fast because it was thin aluminum. I put it right back. One of my daughters came into the kitchen. She was four or five years old. I told her that she could touch the bottom of that pot and it wouldn't hurt her. She knew what hot was and looked at me with a really strange look on her face. Dad was telling her that what she knew for sure about that pot of boiling water wouldn't happen. She shook her head a little. I told her to hold her hand out palm up. She did, but she was really unsure. Ready? I asked. No response, but she was looking very nervous. I put the pot on her hand and then quickly took it away. She looked at me with the strangest look on her face: A mixture of wonderment and relief. I experienced another moment of enlightenment. My child had unbridled trust in me. She knew a pot of boiling water would hurt her, but because Dad said it wouldn't, she let me put that pot on her hand.

I spent the next ten minutes explaining to her that touching a pot of boiling water is not something she should ever do again and that hot is hot.

> *You really have to be careful what you tell your children. The trust they have is boundless, but their understanding is very limited.*

On another day, I watched my wife prepare our kids for school and was impressed. So impressed I thought to pay her a compliment after the kids were gone. "You know, you really take good care of those kids. They're so neat and clean and just good-looking." Her answer, as I look back on things, was the hint that my family life was doomed, but I just didn't know it. "What would people think of me if I didn't?" What? It's not about the kids?

We had a little set of table and chairs in the kitchen for the girls. Cathy, the oldest was sitting there, and for some reason, I asked her which hand was her right hand (she was that young). She gave me that look that a kid can that let me know she didn't know what I was talking about. I went behind her and raised her right hand. "This is your right hand." Then I pointed to her left hand and told her that was her left hand. I asked her several times which hand was left or right. It became almost a game. I sat across from her and raised my right hand and asked her which hand I had up. She said left hand. I said, "No, it's my right hand." And she got this perplexed look on her face, looked at her left hand, and said, "No, that's the left hand." I took her right hand in my right hand and then moved around behind her. The look of understanding she had is burned into my memory, obviously, and I felt warm and fuzzy.

I learned the joy of parents teaching their children.

We bought a house and moved in. We were still in Gibbstown. I set about doing the remodeling that needed to be done in order for the place to be "ours." I stripped the walls of the dining room and the living room and then repaneled them. I finished the den on the main floor and added a bar and a dartboard. After we had two more daughters, I redid the rear entrance into a clothes washing room, and redid the upstairs main bedroom for the three girls. We had a dormer added on upstairs, which added two more rooms up there so it became a two-and-a-half-story building. And then there was the burglar alarm I designed and installed.

Self-taught and OJT skills may help lower costs of house repair and remodeling but doesn't qualify a person for "Professional" licensing.

I tried my hand at coaching baseball. My girls were on the team I coached named the Tiger Kittens. We spent time in the backyard learning how to throw and catch a ball. They also discovered that as long as you have your baseball glove on and held between you and the ball, the ball can't hurt you.

My sports life of softball and darts put too many temptations in my path, and I fell to one. A sweet young thing turned my head. My wife learned of it, and I found my indiscretion brought on real trouble. There were extenuating circumstances to my way of thinking. Bedroom activity wasn't up to the frequency and variety I wanted. I'd brought that up to my wife more than once. She'd finally told me she was the way she was, and I just had to live with it. So I shut up.

Our tenth wedding anniversary was approaching, and I proposed that we get married again to mark the change and dedication I was prepared to make. This idea was soundly rejected, so I shut up.

I talk about these things because one part of my life was not going well.

I found out there were severe penalties that came with adultery.

Over the next few years, as my entire vocational environment changed, things were very cool between my wife and me. I went from structured work conditions in one place to flying all over North America and being away from home for a week or two at a time. She told me the kids didn't need her so much now that they were in High School and she wanted to get a job. So long as the girls didn't come home to an empty house, was my condition. I soon learned that while I was away, she ignored what we'd agreed to; and not only wasn't she home when school let out, she was out a lot at the bar in a local motel.

One night after league darts, one of my friends approached me in a very cautious way. He informed me that my wife was seeing some bartender. I understood his cautiousness. This was a very touchy subject. I went to the bar I was told about and confronted the guy. He was correctly concerned for his welfare. When I asked if he loved her, there was reluctance. When asked if he wanted her, there was more reluctance. When asked if his wife knew, he got a panicked look on his face. The conditions for him not having to be concerned for his welfare were explained to him. Take her that night, and the kids would have to be part of the bargain because she'd insist on having them, or call her right then and tell her he never wanted to see or talk to her again, without mentioning he'd met me. He opted for the phone call.

The situation in my home had become nasty, to the point where I packed a bag and moved to a little room over a bar. I was living on cheese steak sandwiches. One night, while sitting at the bar, I got into a discussion about what was going on and gained a really great insight into what was happening. My wife, with support from at least one of her friends, had seen a lawyer and had a separation agreement drawn up. Every time I saw or heard from her, she informed me of something else that was added to the separation agreement. It dawned on me that these negotiations were going the way they were because she had nothing to lose. I needed to change that. I took my bag and returned to the house. In an indignant tone of voice, she asked what I was doing. She learned that I was prepared to live there, right alongside of her in bed, for the next twenty years if needed be. The world outside of the house would see me being contrite and humble. She would have to live with that condition unless I could at least look forward to a semblance of a life worth living. She believed me.

I knew what it cost to maintain the house and agreed to send her enough money to keep home and hearth intact, with some left over for the girls, but she would have to supply the money for whatever extras she wanted. The thought of having to live with me in the house was the incentive she needed. I moved into an apartment.

Every month I wrote a check; I never missed. Years later, I learned the girls weren't getting any of the money. I started writing checks to each of the girls in addition to the one for the house upkeep. I found out she was cashing those checks too. The girls did not know of my efforts on their behalf.

# DARTS

By this time, I had three girls, and I was looking for ways to bring in more money. I built a back porch for a friend of my wife's with the knowledge I'd gotten from working with my dad. I did some house repair work on windows and doors for a family who heard I was a handyman kind of person.

I designed a burglar alarm system and installed it in our house from parts I got from the plant. The day after that was installed, I was in Philly looking to hustle some money playing darts and feeling really good about myself. We called the guy who owned the bar, Patches. "What do you look so happy about?"

I told him how comfortable I was that my house was protected while I was away. He gave me an

"Oh Yeah?" That was more a sarcastic remark than a comment.

"What?" I asked him.

"Nothing" came back.

"You think I can't put in a burglar alarm?"

"You know how I got the money to buy this bar?" he asked.

"No, what's that got to do with anything?"

"I used to be a thief."

"Yeah, sure you were."

"I'd set your alarm off on my way out of your house with everything you own."

"Get out of here."

"You have switches on the ground floor windows and doors, right?"

"Yeah," I said, "so what?"

"I was what people call a second-story man. They called us that because that's how we'd go into a house, through the second-floor windows. My partner and me would drive around looking for a place that looked like it had expensive stuff in it, and then wait for the right time to go in. Holidays were good times."

"When they'd be throwing a party, we'd park in the next block and go around back looking for which room upstairs had a light on. That would be the bathroom, and the window next to that would be the master bedroom, where their best stuff and the guests' coats would be. We'd get their ladder from the garage and put it up. One of us would go into the bedroom and empty the drawers from dressers and stands beside the bed into the pillowcases and throw them down. We'd throw down any fur coats too."

"On nights when there wasn't anyone home we'd hit the downstairs and go right for the freezers, because that's where the jewelry would be. We'd leave the house out the back door. That's when I'd be setting off your alarm that you're so happy about."

"Damn, Patches. You make me feel like there's nothing I can do about this stuff."

"Good insurance will do it. On a good haul, we'd wait for a couple of months and then go back and hit it again. The insurance would have put all new stuff back in the house by then."

I did a burglar alarm system for a neighbor, which I got paid for, but I never told them what Patches told me.

My job was going along pretty well: raises regularly, on the BOD of the CIU, given projects to develop and complete on my own, and compliments from my Foreman on the work I was doing. I had a cushy assignment of working in the shop overhauling and calibrating instruments. No more standing on the top of eighty-foot towers trying to thaw out frozen transmission tubing with a steam hose in the middle of the night.

The first time I picked up a dart was in Billy Burt's, the local watering hole.

Draft beer was ten cents and if you brought your own jug, you could buy a gallon of beer for a dollar.

Billy Burt's wasn't fancy, but a place where you could sit at the bar, have a few drinks and talk with friends. There was an old pot belly stove and just behind that, an American dart board. This was a place to shoot darts. No one actually owned a set of darts back then. They used the bar darts.

The construction of the board made bounce outs a frequent problem. Somehow, someone discovered that if you stuck the tip of the dart into a raw potato, it would give the dart a better chance of sticking. Occasionally, a bet was made that the loser had to eat the potato, no matter how old it was. I joined several leagues and as I gained experience I discovered I had a knack for the game.

I found a new way to bring in money—hustling at darts.

I joined a team in Philly in 1973, through Bob Thiede. It was the Manor Bar.

Bob Thiede, Lenny Craig, Dick Yost, Norm Finley, Bud McDonald, John Sheridan, Lenny Macy, Charles Ochichnowski, Bob Miller, Bill Samuels, and Mac Namara were on the roster. This was a pretty good bunch of players.

I'd seen a few Philly players at tournaments, and some in a couple of bars where I'd been "visiting." I had some luck finding people to play against in a couple of places, so I thought I'd try going over to Philly again. There were so many bars and dart players over there that I figured this could be a pretty good pond in which to fish. Not so many people knew me, so I might have some fun.

Here's something you should know about me augmenting my income through darts: It was sort of like freshwater fishing, as opposed to salt-water fishing. In fresh water, you can pretty much narrow down which kind of fish you are likely to hook if you pay attention to some things. If trout is your kind of fish, you start looking in trout streams, for bass you look in lakes, for catfish you look in slow-moving mucky water, and so forth. In salt water, if you stay "inside"—that's inlets, sounds, and marshes—you can pretty much limit the kinds of fish you might hook; but if you go outside, you are limited to bottom fishing or trolling to try for specific types of fish. In salt water, outside, you never know what will jump on your hook. Okay, you get my drift. So, there is a certain level of dart player I liked to find when fishing for dart players. The intention was not to pump up my ego or work on my emotional practice; it was to pick up a few bucks, and I wanted to do it at as little risk as possible. I needed to select the pond carefully since each pond has a big fish in it, and that fish was my target; but I didn't want a shark in the way. Plus, in smaller towns, word got around pretty fast, and return trips to the pond might be spoiled. I didn't figure Philly as one big pond, but as a bunch of smaller ones, neighborhood ponds, where I might be able to go fishing for a very long time.

Getting the fish to nibble at my bait was an art. The life of a darts fisher is limited in any case, because as soon as you are recognizable, the game is up. Word gets around very fast. Winning at prestigious tournaments didn't help with staying under the radar, and I had been doing that; but they were all out of town, and Philly darts people knew very little outside of what happened in their neighborhood if it didn't have anything to do with someone they knew, so I had been able to skate out of sight. Just another guy that showed up and got lucky then disappeared again. No one knows where he's from, nobody cares.

Self-preservation required me to be adept at not making those who lost to me angry, which is a skill all by itself. I say this because I liked the game and the people in it and wished to be involved in league and social play on an ongoing basis if I couldn't "fish" anymore. Sort of having my cake and eating it too.

I certainly wanted to avoid playing against the best people at the game. That would have been counter to my goal and unnecessarily put winning at risk.

Knowing all the above, one Saturday, I was headed for Philly to see what I could drum up, so I figured I'd stop in the Manor Bar to check it out.

Hard to find a parking place; they must be giving away beer in this place. (I found out later there was some kind of tournament being played.) *It looks promising*, I was thinking. I walked in. Nice place. Pretty clean and lots of people at the bar and dart cases all over the bar too. These were dart people! A couple of dartboards, but no one playing. This was looking better all the time. I took a seat and looked around. A few stools down was a guy I'd met at a couple of tournaments. His name was Ray Fischer. I figured that meant the end for my fishing trip since this guy was one of the best in the country. As I looked around, I noticed there were a number of guys in that place that were highly ranked countrywide. At that time, the center of dart expertise in America was the Delaware Valley (Philly and its suburbs, which included Southern Jersey). The guys in Philly thought it only included Philly. I was going to get a Coke and then quietly head for some other place. I nodded in recognition to Ray.

Ray was the butt of some good-natured ribbing going on. A group of guys wanted to play partners for some money, and as they were choosing, they kept at Ray to pick somebody. Afraid to lose? Worried the moths will get out of your wallet? Nobody wants to be your partner? These kinds of things were being tossed around amid raucous rounds of laughter. After a couple of minutes, it didn't look as though Ray was enjoying it all that much. We caught eyes, and Ray mouthed, "Want to play?" A quick glance told me no one saw the exchange. Here was Ray Fischer, one of the best, asking me if I wanted to be his partner against this collection of high-powered shooters. How could a guy not jump at that chance? I nodded. Ray waited a few minutes, and then he said in a nice strong voice, "Okay, I'll take that kid." And he nodded in my direction.

You're probably ahead of me on this, but, my name was never mentioned. The others there didn't recognize me. They didn't think of me as anyone to be particularly concerned about. After all, I wasn't from Philly, and they didn't know me, so how good could I be?

We played, and as with a lot of neighborhood bars, especially one owned by a dart player, (this one was owned by Charlie Young, one of the better players), people would borrow money from the owner and put an IOU in the cash register to be paid later. As teams would either run out of money, or run up enough IOUs, they dropped out. We were playing heads up, teams, winner kept the board, loser got back in line to challenge.

It got late; it was nearly closing time for Charlie, although if dart activity was hot and heavy, he'd just lock the door, and the play would continue. Someone asked Charlie for some more cash to get into the next game, and Charlie said, "I gotta close." This was out of the ordinary. Charlie explained, "There isn't any more cash in the register, only IOUs." And he looked over at Ray and me. No mystery where all the money was. It was there with the two guys with the big grins on their faces.

Two things ended when Charlie had to close on time: the dart matches that night and my ability to wander around in NE Philly unnoticed on fishing trips. That part of Philly was really a big little town.

Camden, New Jersey, is a city that has changed a lot and like all the other cities, neighborhoods are bounded by streets. Most of the time, they are four or five blocks in size, sometimes bigger, sometimes smaller, depending upon the city. As with most neighborhoods, the demographics changed from one neighborhood to the next, but in the sixties, there weren't all that many mixed neighborhoods. One is Italian, next might be Polish or Irish or Chinese or

African American or some other ethnicity. And there were different kinds of bars within each neighborhood.

There were lots of places where a guy would go with a date or his wife or look for some female to meet. Nice places, clean places, places with dart teams and pool teams and shuffleboard teams, and things like that. And there were bars and saloons, which also had the same types of games in them, but a guy would never think of taking a "nice" girl or wife into such a place. These were rough-and-tumble joints, mostly. They were rough-and-tumble mainly because of one element of society that frequented these places. The streetwise types, the muscle beer types, the motorcycle gang types, and the just-plain-gang types. One thing about the kinds of people who hung out in those places: they were gamblers. Not to suggest that there wasn't gambling in all the other bars and taverns, but these folks would bet on anything, anytime, and they had no sense about money. That was the distinguishing feature most of them shared. They would collect their weekly pay from whatever they were doing; mostly, payday was Friday, but sometimes Saturday, depending on if they worked Saturday, because if it were any other day, a number of them wouldn't show up for work the following day. In they come with their cash or check and, first things first, would pay off their bar bill. The owners of the bars knew their clientele, and that was a condition of letting a person run a bar bill. By the time they left the bar on payday, a goodly percentage of them would have little or no money left. They'd spend it on over drinking and buying others drinks and betting on about every game that was in the bar or on sports pools. If they couldn't play the game, they'd start betting on those who were, if it were a decent match.

So, given this information, what's a simple guy who loves to play the game of darts for fun, and sometimes use money as a way to keep score of who won the most games, to do? Not a lot of the upper-level darts guys frequented these rough-and-tumble places, so the poor things in these places were left to pass their money around to each other. Someone had to help with this situation, and being the Good Samaritan that I was, I accepted that responsibility.

So it came to be that I walked into a bar in the Kramer Hill section of Camden, New Jersey, in 1970. I don't remember the name of the place. There were two doors, one from the back parking lot and one from the street, on opposite sides of the building. From the back door entrance, as you entered, there was a dartboard on the wall to the left, and a bar along the wall on the right. There were restroom entrances at the far end of the bar, booths along a wall that was half the length of the bar and one wall of the restrooms, with not much room between the barstools and the booths. A pool table was directly ahead just off another wall, which was this side of the restrooms.

Two guys at the bar, one on a stool and the other standing and talking to the one seated. The one standing had that look of a wiry, quick, and strong guy. His shoulders sloped, and his arms were well toned. He had that demeanor about him that shouted "Street wise."

Belly up to the bar, draught Bud, I say. This was no place to order a Coke if you didn't want to get noticed. I lit a Chesterfield, leaned on one elbow, and turned my attention to the dart set up behind me.

"You play?" came from the guy standing.

"Yeah, I like the game. You?"

"I'm on a team, in the league. I'm not as good as I used to be, I've been away from the game for a while." "

Wanna play? I say.

"Yeah. I'm Jim," he says.

"George," I say." Something about Jim that struck me the right way. I liked the guy. We played one game of everything counts for six innings, and I won by a few points.

"Want to play for something?" Jim says.

"Sure," I say. "A beer?" I asked.

"Yeah," Jim says. We play and I win, and I saw Jim was not very good at this. His stroke was short, his body lunged just a touch, and he couldn't group his darts worth a hill of beans. Since I'm such a nice guy, and I liked this guy, I decided to put my fishing pole away. I backed off enough to have the games go back and forth.

"You're good at darts, huh," Jim says. Since I'm being nice, "Yea, I am, I say." Somehow, Jim sized the situation up, an instinct from the street I guess. "Looking for a money game, huh?" I nod, "Not so's anybody should know," and smile. We connected.

"Anybody come in here that plays for a few bucks that I should know about?" I say.

"Some," Jim said. "Maybe somebody will show up." We talked about the league, and Len Craig and other people for a while." Jim looked past my shoulder and said, "Here come a couple of guys who play a lot in here." I cast a casual glimpse, and we continued talking while the two guys got into a dart game. Jim told me he knows them by sight but hadn't played them. Jim says, "Wanna try 'em?"

"Partners," I say.

Jim got us into the game. We played a couple of games for drinks, and it looked as though we needed to call games that favor having one strong partner, so I quietly suggested that to Jim. After a few more games, which went back and forth, I quietly asked Jim, "Which one will go for a few games single—O? Jim tells me. "We're partners all night, right, I say? And we both know how we wanted this to work. I would get to the right guy eventually, and we'd split the winnings.

"How about we play for a buck a game," Jim asked?

I'd been playing a reserved game, winning when I had to, letting Jim win the game for us when he could, just pacing and sizing things up. Like, which innings does this guy prefer, and which games would he rather play? I was nursing my beer, back turned to the board, when I heard raised voices. Jim and the two guys had a disagreement over a shot that was made, or not, and eyes became locked over the exchange. Now, I didn't want to lose a chance at a few bucks, and this setup was too good to lose. I could beat this guy without even breaking a sweat, so I had to resolve this quickly. Jim had the darts in his hand, and I saw him put them down while looking at one of the guys. I knew what was coming. Both those guys were bristled. Not a good thing.

I stepped about half way toward the other team. "I got this, Jim. Don't worry about it," I said. I turned to the two guys, and Jim stalked off to the bar far enough to be out of reach but close enough to where he could get right back if needed. I learned what the disagreement was, understood I could handle the situation, and let them have their way. Then I took my turn and made the shot, a difficult one it was, and that ended the game.

We played only a couple of more games before the others quit playing and left the bar. Jim and I split the few bucks we had, got a couple of more beers, and then I left, saying I had a few more stops to make before I called it a night.

Not being one to shirk my responsibilities, I returned to that bar again the next week. Jim was there. He greeted me like some long-lost brother. There were maybe a dozen people in the place, and he told everyone: "This is George, and he's my friend." He guided me to one of the booths. He instructed the barmaid: "George doesn't pay for anything tonight." *Wow, because we won a few dollars? This is strange. Great—but strange.*

We sat and began talking,-well, me mostly listening. Jim unloaded. He was the King of Kramer Hill, he told me. He owned this place, he said in a matter-of-fact tone. One of the women at the bar got up and headed toward the restrooms. The distance from the booth table to the bar was only a couple of feet, and as she got even with us, Jim planted his foot against the bar, blocking her way. "You want a girl tonight," he asked me?

I didn't know what to say.

Jim didn't wait. "How 'bout her? She looks good, huh?"

This woman was with some dude at the bar, so I knew this was going to get real bad, real fast. I looked up at the woman. She was standing stark still, her hands just above Jim's leg, but not touching. She had a frightened look on her face. Then here comes the guy, and trouble. The guy walked the few feet down the bar in our direction, but just as he came near, Jim stopped him. All Jim did was look at the guy and say, "Sit your ass back down."

The guy backed up to his stool and sat. The woman stood without a movement.

In a flash, I understood what he'd said. He owned this place—which had nothing to do with proprietorship of this bar or Kramer Hill. Jim was a genuine badass. And I was his friend. Therefore, whatever I wanted to do had his blessing. *Oh my God, how do I get out of this?*

"Thanks Jim. I appreciate this, but I'm really not in the mood. I'm looking for some dart action."

His reaction was something else. "Sure. That's cool." He dropped his foot; the woman forgot about going to the restroom, turned, and walked straight out the back door with her guy right behind her. As if nothing happened, Jim took up talking again. "We're low on beer here," he said, and two showed up right quick. We visited in Jim's "place" for an hour or so, and I learned what he meant by what he'd said the first time we met. He had been away from darts for a while. Yeah, in the slammer for murder was why he'd been away. He'd beaten some poor sap to death. Somehow his conviction had been overturned, and he was now out. It had been his second conviction. He told me some about his history, and wasn't bragging about it. He showed me his hands as he talked about, why he couldn't play darts all that well. The knuckles were all lumpy and a bit crooked. Got that way from punchin' guys out, he explained. Seems he picked up money by helping collect overdue "loans" once in a while, among other odd-job kinds of things. He was telling me things that could have been true, but I knew for certain he was the genuine article.

As I sat listening, I was wondering what had happened that put me on such a high scale with him. A dart game? Doesn't seem likely. Then it struck me. I had told Jim I'd take care of a problem for him. Not in those exact words, of course—and certainly not with the intent that Jim attached to it. I'd been talking about handling the dart game situation and Jim thought I meant I would handle the two guys for him. I was protecting the King of Kramer Hill? What kind of badass did he think I was? And more importantly, how could I get out of there without him finding out what a mistake he'd made?

This was one time when being able to hustle really did come in handy. The ability to let someone believe what they wanted to believe, even without facts to support them, can be a blessing. I left and never went back. Jim played one game for Apollo, the team that won the championship that year. Team members Bob Thiede, Joe Dick, and Jack Fletcher all averaged over 50 and Len Craig only averaged 49.91. Jim, in his game, shot 40, and nobody died.

Some years earlier, Babe Kelly's bar was a neat kind of place in a neat kind of city neighborhood. The kind of neighborhood where there were houses, not just row homes. It was 1967. The little neighborhood had become an island of what used to be, surrounded by what it became.

Babe's was easy to see, but hard to get to. Just as you leave the toll booths on the Benjamin Franklin Bridge, in the far right lane—on the way to Philly, not Babe's—if you looked very closely down into the clutter of buildings you could just make out the little front window with the red-and-blue Pabst beer neon sign in it. Hick Wright, Lenny Craig, Norm Craig, Gordon Nelson, Bob Scarduzio, Ted Rzepski, J. Lassman, W. Kingsmore, and Larry Walker were the players on Babe's team that year, and they were winning everything in sight. They even won the league championship.

My team, Riverside Inn, played Babe's team at Babe's place. Needless to say, this being one of my early years in the "Big League," I was pumped that night. Just to be around those guys was exciting. Hick and Lenny were already legends in our dart world. The way our league was set up, our team only played another team once per half season. That's twice per season. And that made these matches a big deal event.

Hick was born old, I think. At least he was old when I met and played against him. Must have been in his sixties? He is also memorable for me because I had managed a 64-point game, which was the highest in league history to that date, and that old man shot a 67 to beat me. And I had to watch. The other time someone did something like that to me, it was a team mate of mine, Harold, "Ducky" Dillon. I had a three-game score of 172, again the highest of the league, and I watched Ducky shoot a staggering 183. Never before, and never again, did that happen!

Hick wore an old cardigan sweater that had holes in the elbows. It was an ugly old thing, all stretched and dangling. He kept a clump of masonry line chalk in the stretched-out, frayed, right pocket, and all around that pocket, the sweater was covered with line chalk. I don't think he ever had it cleaned. I think it was his lucky sweater, like some athletes have socks or underwear or hat. Imposing stature and demeanor, a craggy-lined face, and piercing eyes for a newbie like me all added to the field of intimidation that surrounded him.

That night was a tense thing for me. I got to shoot a couple of games even though I was a rookie on the team, but not without an attitude, mind you. I was respectful of these giants of the game, and I wanted to shoot against Hick after the match but, the poor old thing had to leave before the match ended so he could get to bed. The match ran late, and it was after midnight when it was finally over. Strangely, there were no money games played.

When Babe closed up, he really closed up. There were bars on the windows, and inside the doors. He was a tough old codger. A bar owner all his life, he saw many a hard situation. Someone asked him if he worried about being robbed, what with being practically under the bridge and no streetlights, and certainly no cops patrolling the area. He said his place could only be robbed over his dead body. A few years later, I learned his place had been robbed, just the way he said it would have to be.

What with Babe closing, it being late, and me being excited about the whole match thing, I didn't realize I should have hit the men's room before I started home. I'd hardly got started when I realized I was nearly in an emergency situation. This realization coincided with another realization. I was surrounded by neighborhoods where I would stand out very much were I to get out of my car. There were a lot of very angry people at that time, and there were some of them who wouldn't take kindly to me being in "their" neighborhood. Especially considering what I was in need of doing. A light in a window, dim and bluish, yeah, and it indicated that the kind of facilities of which I was in need would be in that place with that neon sign.

And a parking spot right in front of the place? This had to be divine intervention. I locked the car, mounted the two steps, opened the door, and stepped inside. It was really dingy in there. And smoke-filled. It took a couple of seconds for my eyes to adjust, and when they did, I found there were multiple sets of eyes boring into me. Quick like a bunny, I found the men's room sign and headed for it, feeling the eyes following me. Once inside, with the relief I so desperately needed, I shifted my attention to the sounds coming through the walls. *Thump, thump, thump.* There was something very familiar about those sounds. Darts! That was the sound of darts hitting a dartboard. Now, you can draw whatever conclusion from what I did next, but in retrospect, I've decided I had no common or any other kind of sense at that time. The siren's call was too much for me.

I left the men's room and walked along the bar. It was an oblong affair, passing turning heads and glaring eyes. The wall of the men's room on one short end of the bar. My eyes were adjusted enough to see that the place was about half full of people who didn't seem to be all that pleased I was in there. I walked along the long side on the men's room side, rounded the corner to the other short side of the bar, and then walked along the short side to the next corner and, against every bit of safety sense, walked past the door I should have been nearly running out, to where the darts were being shot at the other end of the bar. I'd walked all the way around the bar in this place, which could be described without exaggeration as dangerous!

The bar had drinks on it indicating the dart players took up the four seats, so I stopped at the next one in line. The bartender came to where I was. It was then I noticed he'd been following me in my trip around the bar. Not a word did he say. He seemed to be trying to figure out if I was insane or some real badass. "Draught" was all I said as I laid a buck on the bar and lit a Chesterfield. I turned my attention to the dart players. There were four of them playing partners, and my intrusion didn't seem to be alarming to them. I watched a few games without incident, but I did notice the bartender seemed to stay close to where I was.

Sizing up the dart situation took my attention completely off my environment. I was next to a dartboard, with people playing who didn't look as though they were all that good, and they were playing for a dollar a team. I could use a couple of dollars, I reasoned; so I went into "Let's get into this game" mode. These kinds of things usually break up at about the time of night it was, so I looked for the signal that my timing was right. It was. I'd just ordered a second beer when one of the players said he'd had enough and was heading out. Here was my opportunity. "I'll take his place if you want to keep playing," I said.

The guy who was leaving shot a glance at me, picked up his change, finished his drink in one gulp, and walked out. The guy without a partner seemed confused about what to do. Not until later did it dawn on me that having a partner like me would be against all this guy's instincts. It'd be too much to handle. He explained that he'd better get on home and then left. The player I'd identified as the big fish of the four seemed to be weighing something. The guy who had been his partner made up his mind by saying it would be okay if Big Fish wanted to play heads up.

"We've been playing for money here," came from Big Fish.

"I can play for a little," I said.

"Half a buck a game," Big Fish virtually demanded. We settled on three inning games and shot the cork. I was in good form. Win one, lose one, win two, lose one, win two, and lose one, and so on. We'd played for close to half an hour, and things were working right along. I wasn't leaving money on the bar since I didn't want anyone to notice how it was going. The guy I was playing just seemed like any other dart player. We didn't talk all that much, but what there was seemed cordial enough. Along with sizing up how much money there was to get and considering raising the stakes if I could, I noticed that he wasn't drinking much. I'd had three beers; they were little 5 oz. draughts, and once the flow begins with that stuff, it comes out as fast as it goes in, so off to the men's room I went.

Again, I was feeling all the eyes in the place following me, but who cares? I was winning some bucks. Once inside, as I leaned against the wall, the sounds from the bar came right through as though the wall wasn't even there.

A voice I hadn't heard before asked, "How're you doin' with that, boy?"

Then the voice of the guy I was playing answered. "I'm down some. That boy can play a bit."

Then the strange voice again: "Don't you worry. He won't get out of here with anything."

Sense rushed in all at once, and where I was crashed in, and something close to panic struck. When I walked back around the bar, I was as calm as I had been when I made the trip the other way, as far as anyone could tell. We took up playing again—only this time, I was winning one and losing two. Without anyone noticing, I took cigarettes from the pack and put them in my pocket. It took about fifteen minutes for everything to be right, and the current game ended with me winning. "I've got to run out to my car and get some cigarettes," I said. Half full glass of beer, money, and a crushed, empty cigarette pack on the bar, out I went. "Flew" is a way to describe how I drove from that place. Eyes in the mirror, foot on the floor. There must be a Dart God.

Deep sea fishing takes patience. First, you have to find a spot in the ocean that looks as though there are fish in it. Then you cast your lure and pull it through the spot, being careful not to frighten the fish away, always alert for a strike.

The usual spots where I went looking for fish had been pretty much empty for a couple of weeks, and it was Sunday, the day that fish were hardly ever around, even during good times. I'd heard of a couple of spots that were new to me, up along Route 70 around Marlton. I figured maybe I'd try there sometime even though it was outside my usual area for trolling.

Something about South Jersey you should know: This area I'm talking about is due east of Philly, just across the Delaware River. First places you come to on the Jersey side are Gloucester or Camden or Pennsauken or Burlington, depending on which bridge you cross. My hometown, Gibbstown, is about twenty miles or so south of Philly, and it had about 2,500 people in it (only three towns smaller anywhere around), one traffic light, and three bars: Billy Burt's, Cheeseman's, and Kenny's. Gibbstown was on the southernmost end of an area that ran about fifty miles north by thirty miles east where there are towns and towns and towns and more towns; and south or east from Gibbstown, it was farms and orchards with ponds and lakes scattered about. As you drive in the area, you cross from one town to another, and there is hardly ever a sign that tells you which town you are in. This will give you some understanding of the density of people in the area.

Traveling ten miles was a long way through towns. And every town was a unique place, but most of them seemed hooked together; there were no dividing spaces where there were no buildings. Some were tough kinds of places, like Gloucester and Camden; and others were a bit upper class, like Haddonfield and Audubon. This area is packed with people and bars. The time period I'm talking about was through the 1960s, and the only dart game played in South Jersey was the American type of game. It wasn't necessary to travel very far to find a bar and crowd that you'd never seen before.

So it's Sunday; I hadn't found a game outside of league night for a while—what the hell—so off I go looking for the places I'd recently been told about. The town was named Marlton and was about twenty miles away. I drive up Route 130 through Woodbury and to the Ellisburg traffic circle in Bellmawr and then on to Route 70 and through Collingswood and Haddonfield to Marlton. I drove slowly. Looked for the places on both the left and the right since I didn't know where, exactly, they were. I knew the names of the places, but not what they looked like or their addresses. I spotted one. It was on the right, and I was in the left lane and couldn't get across the traffic in the right lane, of course, so I looked for a place to do a U-turn. As I went, I spotted one of the other places, and it was on the other side of the street, right where I'd be turning. I made my U-turn and came to the other place first. Since I was there, why not check this place out?

Not very many cars in the lot, and that was not a good sign. It looked kind of dumpy, but I thought, *Let's see what we have here.* It had a dirt parking lot, door in front on the street side, Schlitz beer neon signs in the window. Inside, it was sort of dingy—TV behind the bar and one person sitting at the bar talking with the barmaid. It was early afternoon, which is not really the best time for fishing. The dartboard was on the other side of the bar where the restrooms were. "Yeah. Hi, just a Coke, thanks," I said to the frumpy-looking barmaid. She had seen her better days. I lit a Chesterfield; half the ashtrays still had butts and ashes in them. The place smelled like stale smoke and beer taps that needed cleaning. It was sort of like the joint was getting over a hangover from the night before. Like this was a nighttime place not used to daylight and didn't like it.

Nothing to do but drink, look at the TV, or talk to the barmaid or the other guy. The guy at the bar had the appearance that most bar flies had at that time of day: rumpled clothes, needed a shave and probably a bath. Shot glass in front of him (half full) and a glass of beer (also half full). Looked like it might be a lively place on the right night, what with tables over by the wall where the restrooms were and a bumper pool table over there too. Shuffleboard behind me along the wall on the street side. It was a hangout kind of place.

I took my Coke around to the dartboard side of the bar. Searched around for the light switch on the dartboard. I was told the barmaid would turn it on. Thanks, I told her. I shot a handful and discovered it really was early afternoon—my arm hardly worked. I'd better throw some to get some kind of stroke. I could pretty much tell this place was not going to pay off. I killed twenty minutes and two Cokes, and then headed for my car.

There was another place just up the street, between where I was headed in the first place and this joint I was just leaving. I pulled into the lot: three cars. Not looking good, but who knows? Same act. "Just a Coke. Thanks," I said to the bartender. There's a dart league schedule on the wall by the dartboard. Hope brightens. I recognized the names of a couple of the bars on the schedule, looks as though Thursday night is the night in this place. I could turn the dartboard light on myself. Three guys at the bar watching TV; one had a bottle of beer and the other two had shot glasses with what looked like water back. Heavy boozers in the afternoon are not dart shooters. The beer guy could be, so let's go into the act. Walk to the dartboard, turn on the light, and shoot a few. Well, they felt better than they did in the other place. The Coke was gone. Order another one?

I said, "No, maybe a small draught beer this time." Can't drink Coke all day. That stuff will get you so wired you can't sleep. That's supposed to be from the cocaine in it, I think. After about another twenty minutes, Beer Guy left. Okay, that's long enough here. Let's go see if there is anything at the place I started for in the first place. Somebody with too much money for the talent they have would probably walk in just after I left. Wouldn't be the first time. I was already thinking about a couple of other places I knew of, but it was just too early in the day for them, even considering the travel time to cover the miles and towns to get to where they were.

Let's see what this place has to offer. It's bigger, paved parking lot, and steps to climb to the door. *Hey, the place looks kind of clean.* "Hi. No, I think I'll just have a Coke. Thanks." There were four guys on the far side of the U-shaped bar; the dartboard was on this side of the bar. Two guys sitting at a table in front of the window about even with the U part of the bar. This looked like it might be one of those days. Maybe I'd just call it quits. But not just yet. Maybe someone would come in.

Over to the dartboard, find the light switch, shoot a couple of hands full, and go back to my seat, which was at the bar about six or eight feet behind where you stood to play. Sip on the Coke, wander back up to the board, putz with the darts, and keep an eye on the guys on the other side of the bar because they'd noticed what I was doing. Back to my seat to look at the TV for a few minutes. Sip some more at the Coke, and then head back to the board. "Pardon me," came from the shorter guy at the table by the window. "Want to play a few games?"

"Sure. Nothing much else to do," I said. "You want to warm up?"

"Nah, I'm not very good, so it won't make much difference."

Oh? OK. Want to shoot the cork to see who calls the game?

"Huh? Yeah, sure." He was not as bad at this game as he seemed to want me to believe. It showed, in the way he was so comfortable.

"I'll give you one," I said, and I was thinking, *Come close to the cork, but don't hit it.*

He missed outside my shot. "Everything counts for six innings?" I asked "Yeah, sure. I'll go second," I said.

"Okay." He shoots two doubles, scored four, with one dart outside the scoring area.

I shoot and hit four too, but one triple and one single with one dart outside the scoring area. He could group two. I couldn't. We took turns for the six innings, both hitting fours and fives; I have one dart missing most of the time. No sign of being able to group three darts from me, or him. I never win by more than three points.

"How about we skip the cork and just play loser first?" I asked.

"All right with me," he said. "You want to play for something?" he asked.

"Oh, I don't know about that," I said.

He shrugged. "Makes it better to play for something. Yeah, I guess."

"How about a drink?" I said.

"I'm full of drinks," he said. "Why not play for the price of a drink or a quarter a game?"

I liked how this was going. It was not so boring now. "Well, I guess that would be better. I can only drink so many myself. I guess a quarter would be all right," I said.

We played the same game again. This time he won by two. "I got ya on that one," he said with a big smile. I give him a quarter.

"You made a couple of good shots," I said. Okay, same game?" I asked.

"How about three innings instead of six?" he said.

"Why not," I said. I shot first, and this game I won, and again it was by three. Gimme my quarter back," I said, and he smiled.

"Same game," he said as he shoots first. I was sizing him up for an increase to 50¢ a game. We played for about fifteen minutes, and then the other guy at the table said, Why don't I get in the game too? No sense just sitting here." The situation changed, big-time.

*Hmm,* I thought. *I'm caught between the two of them. I've seen this before. I need to watch how this goes. I need to be very careful here because this could go a couple of different ways.*

"Okay," said the blond-haired guy (he was the short one who got up first). Did I mention the blond-haired guy spoke with an accent? Sounded like Swedish or something. "Shoot the cork?" he said.

"Sure," I said. Nobody introduced themselves and nobody seemed to mind that we didn't know each other's names. I was liking this more and more.

We played a few games. The dark-haired guy seemed very comfortable around the board, and his stroke was much smoother than the blondie's. I'm about one-quarter up when the dark-haired guy said, "Let's make it fifty cents. Nobody's getting hurt here," Blondie said.

"Okay with me. I guess that would be all right," I said.

I was still working on what was happening here. And we played a few more games. I was now about a dollar up. Blondie said, "I got to go to the men's room."

And Darky said, "C'mon, we don't have to wait for him to come back."

"Yeah, I guess," I said.

We played two games; he got one, I got one. Blondie came back. "I'm tired of playing. I'm going to sit down and have a drink."

It was now me and Darky playing three inning games for 50¢ a game. *Ah, so this is the way this is going*, I thought. I won the next game and the next, then lost the third. Darky was now hitting fives and sixes pretty steadily. You play pretty well, huh? he asked.

"I don't do bad," I said, with just a bit of attitude. Darky heard what he wanted. We played a few more games.

"What do you say we make it a buck?" he said.

I'd seen seed money lost early before. I glanced at the money on the bar by my Coke. "Sure," I said.

Now Darky had heard and seen exactly what he wanted to hear and see. Darky walked to his table, sipped from his drink, and said something to Blondie softly enough that I couldn't hear, while he looked out the window for a few seconds. We played a few more games, and Darky was now hitting sixes and sevens, and my Coke now had more company, in the form of money. And now it was the kind of money that didn't make noise when you dropped it.

Darky walked over to Blondie, spoke to him softly enough that I couldn't hear while he looked out the window and took a sip from his drink. He decided now was the time. I was ready to be hauled in, hook firmly in my mouth. "You're doing very good. How about two?"

I took a drink from my Coke and moved the money on the bar around a bit with one finger. "I can go for that," I said.

Darky was now getting down to it. He was hitting sixes, sevens, and eights in tight little groups of darts, and my Coke was getting more dollars for more company. He was winning games, and often. The ones he was losing were being lost by one, two, or three points. He was just barely out of the money and only needed to improve on that one dart. He also knew I couldn't keep this up and he just needed one more point to change the direction of the flow of money before he tried to raise the stakes.

Darky walked over to his shill. Blondie sipped his drink, looked out the window, and spoke softly to Blondie. Blondie said something to him. Darky came back to the board and made a proposition. "You're getting into me pretty good there, and we're waiting for our dates to show up, so how about giving me a chance to get my money back?"

I touched the money around my Coke. "I can go for that," I said. Two innings for five bucks? Sure, I said. I had now been set up for the kill.

We got to playing. The only words exchanged were ones used to call the game. We were playing winner calls the game and loser first. We played for maybe half an hour. Darky walked over to the table, took a sip of his drink, looked out the window, and spoke softly to Blondie. Blondie said something. Darky said, "I'd like to stay here and clean you out but we have to go get our dates for dinner."

"You're lucky you caught me at a bad time" and "I got to go," came from Darky, with a bite to it. There was nastiness to his tone.

As I toyed a finger around in the money by my Coke, I looked him dead in the eyes. "It's really too bad you have to go," I said. "Too bad you had dates that were supposed to show but now you have to leave to pick them up before I can find out just how much faith your backer has in you."

Blondie and Darky left. As I pulled out of the parking lot, I was thinking about how really effective losing one and winning two is. On another day, I learned from some people in Philly that Wes Keys and his money backer traveled all over Philly hustling, and his big mouth got him in a lot of trouble. And hurt a bit.

In order to hustle somebody, you have to be better at the game than they are.

Fishing on Sunday can be fun—especially when you get to meet a Wes Keys.

I found yet another way to bring in money. I met a guy named Jerry who owned a bar in Gloucester City. It wasn't a high-class place, just a bar. There was another bar downstairs that wasn't being used. I asked Jerry why not, and he said he didn't have a bartender to work it. I volunteered to work it for $20 a night. Jerry's rathskeller opened.

Something about Gloucester: it was a sort of rough town. There was a chapter of the Warlocks Motorcycle Club there. Jerry's bar was one of the very few bars in Gloucester where they could take their girls out for a few drinks; they were flagged from most every place. Jerry had a deal with them, since most of them were Gloucester kids anyway. If they didn't wear their colors, they could come into his bar. So here's the situation: I'm downstairs with a bar full of Warlocks and civilian guys and girls. The regular guys knew the Warlocks from before they were Warlocks and didn't think very much of them. There was bad blood between these people. One night I heard a rumpus outside and went up to see what was happening. Out in the street, there were fists flying all over the place. I could hear the sirens of cop cars coming. That was kind of how things could get in Gloucester sometimes.

The rathskeller was working out very well, and I had a busy bar every Saturday night and was making some extra money.

This one night, I was working my butt off and heard the tear of paper. There were posters on the walls, and one of the most weak-minded of the clientele had ripped one down and was stuffing it into his boot. Me not being the brightest bulb in the pack came out from behind the bar and grabbed the guy by the shirtfront while explaining to him in terms he'd understand that he had to vacate the premises. One of the regular Gloucester guys shouted at me, "Watch his hand!" The guy had a carpet knife in the air. He wasn't able to handle me in any way, and in the short tussle, he got nicked by his own knife. I showed him the door in a direct way, and unfortunately, his face got to the door first. The place calmed down quickly, and the night went on.

The next week, I came into work and the place was empty—not a soul. Jerry and his brother were at the end of the bar, but that was it. Jerry's brother was wearing a sports jacket, which was really strange. "Where's everybody," I asked. Word had gotten out about my handling of the jerk the week before, and it turned out the Warlocks had a rule that if any of their people were mistreated, the whole bunch would exact penalty on the offending parties. Jerry heard we might be visited by the Warlocks. I then knew why Jerry's brother was wearing a sports jacket. Jerry handed me a scrap of paper with a phone number on it and a dime. He told me that if he called down to me, I was to call the number on the paper and beat it out of there through the side door without waiting for someone to answer the phone. There was a truckload of people a short distance up the street in a bar in Camden waiting for the phone to ring. They were friends of a friend of Jerry's from South Philly.

I went on down and opened the rathskeller. Around ten o'clock, it was just me in there with my paring knife. I heard voices from upstairs and gripped my paring knife and dime. I heard footsteps on the stairs. It was Bolt and Peggy—people who knew the workings of Gloucester. Half an hour later, the place was packed. I later learned the guys from Philly were carrying more than paring knives, and that I'd just missed a very bad experience.

I figured my life as a bartender was over. Instead, the father of Jerry's friend owned an upscale nightclub in Runnemede named the Rainbow Room, and I could work there if I wanted. I think Jerry later made a deal with the Warlocks to get me out of his place, and his friend got me a job in the Rainbow Room.

*It pays to know people.*

My job in the Rainbow room required me to run a service bar until the main sixty-seat bar and the tables filled. I had to wear a tuxedo jacket when I opened my twelve-seat bar to take care of the overflow.

It was early one night, around nine thirty, and Jim, the owner, told me to open my bar. We were nearly empty, so

I asked Jim what was up and was told to just open the bar. I did. A few minutes after I opened, three guys walked across the bridge from the entrance. There was a waterfall down the wall by the entrance, and the water ran in a little ditch between the main bar and the dance floor. There was a bridge over the ditch. The two bigger guys took seats at either end of my bar, and the older guy sat in the middle seat. The big guy on my right ordered a mixed drink—I don't remember what—and when I made it, he directed me to serve it to the guy in the middle. I did. They hung around for maybe fifteen minutes. The big guy dropped a bill on the bar and told me to keep it, and they left. Jim told me to close my bar and go back to the service bar. I didn't ask who that was; I didn't want to know who that was.

I made very good money at the Rainbow Room, and most of it came from working the rathskeller bar that opened just before the main room closed. Friends of Ralph's (Jerry's friend and the son of the owner) would close their places in South Philly and then come over and play craps on the pool table in the rathskeller until the sun came up.

*The money a job pays isn't all that matters.*

I'd come to a state of mind about my life. I'd decided there were three parts to it: my job, my family life, and my darts life. As long as two out of the three were doing all right, I could be happy.

# The 1970s

# JOB CHANGE AND RELOCATION

The principal product of the Repauno Works was moved to North Carolina, and the plant went from 3,000 employees to 300. Because I was an instrumentation trained person, instead of being laid off, I was recruited into a new business that DuPont was getting into as a sales service representative (SSR). The corporation became involved in the radiology business with a new concept of X-ray film; one that did not need a darkroom. It was called the Dupont daylight system.

*Having a trade is a good thing.*

My territory was Southern New Jersey; Eastern Pennsylvania; Maryland; Washington DC, and Virginia.

My job was principally servicing equipment, assuring those who bought the daylight system that they'd made a good choice. My tool to do that was keeping the machines running trouble free. There were engineers at the manufacturing plant in Delaware, who were the backup resource for field SSRs when we got in over our head.

I was working on a malfunctioning machine in a hospital in Washington, DC, when the requirements of my job really came home. I started on that machine midafternoon, and the problem was an intermittent one. It would work, and then it wouldn't, and then it would—the worst kind of malfunction.

I was sitting on the floor of the X-ray room, parts of the machine littered around me; and it was nine o'clock at night. All the engineers had gone home. There were patients scheduled for X-rays one after another beginning at seven thirty in the morning and continuing throughout the entire day.

This service call became my service epiphany. The machine was virtually dismantled; the schematics were spread around on the floor. I was the one with the responsibility to fix this situation. I was on my own. I studied the schematics more closely and with a different attitude and identified the part most likely to cause the symptoms. I fixed the problem. When I walked out of that hospital, I'd become a professional service representative.

> *A professional understands the concepts of his vocation—the hands-on tools and non-hands-on aspects and how to use those to work his way out of unusual situations—in any field of endeavor.*

## Cleveland

I did what was needed to do my job and help the TRs (technical representatives) with theirs, plus more. I received a promotion, which required me to relocate to Cleveland, where I worked closely with the sales team there. I was in a sales division and worked in support of TRs as they worked against offers from a competitor: Kodak.

*Taking initiative can be a good thing.*

My job changed entirely. I became an SSR with emphasis on sales. A Sales Service Representative complete with a company car, an expense account, a territory to manage, and customers and TRs to keep happy, and the freedom to run my territory as I saw fit.

I worked at another part of my SSR job that most did not: Sales. Not direct sales, just a part of sales. This I found out was a skill set with which I had no experience. I thought like Popeye: I am what I am, and that's all what I am. I had yet to learn that the kind of sales I was involved in was mostly influencing people's decision making.

*You can't force a person to change their mind. You have to influence the way they think so they will decide in the direction you want them to go.*

I acquired knowledge on tricks and tactics by paying close attention to the best salespeople we had.

There was, and still is, a strong rivalry between college football fans. People either loved or hated the University of Michigan or Ohio State University. The decision maker at a hospital in Ohio, who was a customer of Kodak's, was a rabid OSU fan. The salesperson for us, DuPont, while trying to get on the good side of this decision maker, mentioned that he was a graduate of OSU and his brother was backup quarterback under Coach Woody Hayes. The decision maker was duly impressed. When asked if he'd like an autograph from Woody Hayes, the decision maker said that if the sales person could pull that off, he'd switch to DuPont products. He was given a football with Woody Hayes's signature, and we got the business. It could have been signed by Woody Hayes, or by the backup quarterback. Doesn't really matter; both people were happy.

From my apartment, I could see one of the hospitals that had our Daylight system. It was Friday, and I was doing paperwork to clean up for the weekend and have a short day. When I checked for messages, I had a call for service from that hospital. While looking at the window to his office, I called the Chief and asked him to keep what I was going to do for him between him and me because I could get in trouble if people found out. I said I'd leave what I was doing, get him up and running, and then come back to what I was doing. He thought I was in another hospital, and I didn't correct him. I was finishing up the work that needed to be done when the chief came into the room and thanked me for putting him ahead of the other hospital and getting his department up and running first. Chalk one up for me and DuPont.

*Doing favors, even if only perceived, goes a long way.*

I'm driving toward Youngstown, coming from Toledo. I live in Cleveland, which is between the two cities! Here is another day which is going to be a long one, two hours to get to Toledo and three hours to get to Youngstown, then another hour to get home. *Damn,* I think. Then, out of nowhere comes this recall of something that happened when I was working at the Repauno Plant: peanut butter and jelly.

In the instrument shop, as usual, it was time for lunch. It happened at the same time every day, just part of the routine; but this day brought with it one of those flashes of recognition, of understanding, which comes along every so often. Everyone who worked in the instrument shop grabbed their lunch pails and took seats around the large table at the back of the shop. We were hungry, and what was there to be found in that pail amounted to a pleasant surprise, sometimes. I found a thermos of soup, Ritz crackers, and squares of cheese with which I could make little accompaniments for the soup. This break from the usual was a nice thing.

All except one found nothing remarkable enough to make any comment, but this one guy muttered, "Peanut butter and jelly again," which caught our attention. Another guy, seizing on an opportunity to bust on someone, as was the case all the time with this bunch, cracked: "Hey, henpecked, you afraid to tell the little woman to pack something else? We all waited for the reply, and it came: "I pack my own lunch." A silence fell like a pall. No one found anything to say that would add to how dumb this guy just said he was.

Recalling this, I said to myself, *You make your own schedule. What's the matter with you?*

From that day on, I've had a category into which to put things I do to myself that makes my day worse: Peanut butter and jelly.

> *Missing a deadline or goal that doesn't mean anything to anyone but you is not something to get worked up over.*

One of the difficulties with the Daylight machines was the people who used it. They were X-ray technologists, and nearly everyone was a female. They were very competent at their technologist work, but mostly weren't mechanically inclined, and didn't take criticism well. Under the pressure of their workload of patients scheduled for X-rays, they would sometimes put a cassette in the machine with the input end down when it had to be up for the film to drop in. That being the case, when they rotated the handle that moved the cassette up, so the film would fall in, nothing happened. Instead of checking for an error they may have been making, they pushed very hard against the handle, which would break the machine. There were other such things they were doing. So, how do I tell them it wasn't the machine but the way they were using it without making an enemies? The radiologists were constantly haranguing them about not having studies, which were readable, and that was bad enough. I needed to be on their side.

I made cardboard cutouts of techs. There was one boy and one girl. The names of the cutouts were Mr. and Ms. Use. I made a slideshow of the most common mistakes being made with the cutouts peeking from behind the machine. It wasn't the technologists' fault; it was Mr. and Ms. Use. The message was delivered, the machine abuse stopped and the technologists had a good time watching the slide show and eating doughnuts without admitting they were making those errors.

I told the TR what I was going to do and he took the pictures. We shared the credit. The District Manager thought the show childish, not professional, and didn't like it. We received little recognition, and what there was came as less praise than derision. The farther you get from front line workers, the less sense of humor you find.

> *Be very careful when trying to be lighthearted around Supervisors.*

The Supervisor of SSRs was someone I knew from Gibbstown. We went to school together. When he took a position as TR, he recommended me as his replacement for SSR Supervisor. I choose to believe my work with customers, TRs, and equipment was the reason for my promotion.

# DIVORCE

If there ever was such a thing as a manual for how to be a Dad, I didn't know about it. What I have since learned from the study of Managing Behavioral Change would have been useful then, although much of what I did was the right thing to do.

The self-appointed authority on rearing children, when we needed an authority, was Dr. Spock, a man who never lived in a house with children of his own. How he was accepted by the world of people who set forth experts on everything, I'll never know.

I learned what I didn't want to do through watching their Mother. I saw her slap one of our girls in the face because she did something she wasn't supposed to. It made her angry. As soon as the kids were out of earshot, I told her, with emphasis, I never wanted to see her do that again.

A man has physical strength that I believe is a good thing. His instinct is to react to frustration physically. His wife, like his children, should harbor a level of concern for provoking him to a point where he may lose control and react with his physical strength when it's not appropriate. His strength of character keeps his physical strength under control. His wisdom comes from knowing how to avoid a situation where he may be driven to lose control. Confrontation between men brings forth the lessons learned about pecking order back in grammar school. Society's rules frustrate his instinct during confrontations between a man and a woman by denying those lessons. A wife who has decided her man is the cause of her unhappiness can easily put thoughts of using physical strength into his head.

Making the decision for what style of discipline he is going to use is something a Dad needs to do before it becomes necessary to discipline his children.

He pretty much should know what options are available. There is a school of thought that maintains a parent should reason with a child over what is acceptable behavior. That may work if the child understands reasoning. I maintain physical discipline is required when a child has not reached the point where they understand reasoning. Although times have changed, this was acceptable back in my time. That point was different for each of my daughters, but I found out they learned from seeing what their sisters got, so it does kind of happen all at once. I paddled their behinds more than once, and did it just hard enough to jolt their young butts into knowing I was not happy with what they did, or didn't do. Just the fact that Dad was doing this imprinted that they were being disciplined. I never touched them while I was angry. I always waited until I had calmed down but never disappointed them by letting the butt smack not happen. That period of time is what I think had the most impact on them.

When a child reaches an age where reason can be used, something along the line of aversive results from being out of line is what I found to be effective. An example I stumbled upon was TV. One of my daughters had some shows she just loved. Beyond, yelling, fuming, or striking, there was "No TV," and that worked just fine.

Somehow, my experience says, a parent has to outthink a child, and has to know which squabble is a good one to fight and which one is a waste of time and effort. Kids will constantly test their boundaries, so reacting to every instance would be an ongoing thing, so let the little ones go. Don't even bother. "Don't play with the phone cord" is a bad fight. "Stop—don't move," when a child is about to step into a street with traffic, is a good one.

"Just wait until your father gets home; I'm going to tell him about this," was something I didn't take to early on. I felt it made me out to be an ogre and something to be feared, which I didn't want to be. As I slowly grew into Dadhood, I changed my mind. I reasoned that all through this young person's life, there was going to be a rules enforcer father figure. This would be the police in the final analysis, but also the school principal, or boss, or bank manager, as life goes on, and learning there will always be a rule enforcer will stand a young person in good stead.

Mom was with the kids a lot more than Dad, and they could wear her down much faster than they could Dad, so the role of rules enforcer was a good one. "Rules enforcing should not be done in anger but always be done" turned into my mantra. The approach I took brought me rewards from my daughters years later, such as these:

"You must love us more than my friend's Dad loves her. He lets her do whatever she wants." A call while she was in a grocery store: "I'm stuck on a rock in the river of life and just wanted to know what you think about it."

I have one outstanding regret from the separation and divorce mess. I left my children with their mother.

I believed I was the better parent, but the way the law saw it was altogether different. The man in the fight was the automatic loser. The woman has first dibs on the kids and home and the opportunity to tell the story the way she wants the kids to understand it after he is out of the picture.

While still in Cleveland, when I sued for divorce, I took this into consideration as I negotiated the terms of the divorce. I made what I thought to be prudent sacrifice for peace of mind, in order to have it all finished before I returned to New Jersey.

# DARTS IN CLEVELAND

Early in the '70s, a new version of the Dart game was brought to my attention: English Darts. There was a new twist to this game. There was something called out shots. In order to win a game, a person's last scoring dart had to be in a double bed. This required learning combinations of values of the different sections of the dartboard, from one time to two times and three times.

I became the President of the South Jersey English Dart Association, and as such, I wrote an out shot chart of the 170 numbers for which there are combinations of singles, triples, and doubles, which would allow a person to win a game.

In 1972, I joined the Washington Area Darting Association, since I was in that town so often doing my SSR work; and in 1973, I joined the United States Darting Association.

In 1973, I won my first National Dart Tournament in Boston. In my Darts life, I had the highest average and was recognized as the best player in the two leagues in which I played, was the President of one league, won my first national title, and had been given a one-of-a-kind poster designed specifically for, and right off the wall of, the Townhouse Hotel's Bull & Finch Pub, who sponsored the tournament. As an aside, the Bull & Finch Pub became the template for the TV show *Cheers*.

Later in the '70s, I was transferred by my job to Cleveland, Ohio. I immediately sought out Darts activity and joined the Cleveland Dart Club (CDC).

I met a guy named John Grey. John is a different kind of fella. He sought me out and came knocking on my door one night. He just wanted to meet me. We became good friends. John had a drag racing car at one time. He was a bowler and had a couple of 300 games to his credit. He became accomplished at pool and played the guitar, and he was an audiophile. He was one who appreciated the next level up, and after thinking about it for a while, I'd come to understand that he was seeing that in my dart game. It was that it was above ordinary that he enjoyed.

I'd met my dart team mate soon after I arrived in Cleveland. He was a street kind of guy. He lived with an attractive girlfriend who was a street kind of girl.

There was a football player on the Houston Oilers football team who was a very fast-running back, and he wore white shoes. His nickname was Billy White Shoes Johnson. The Bill Johnson I knew wore blue sneakers, so his nickname was Billy Blue Shoes.

Billy Blue Shoes had income from places I knew nothing about, and didn't want to know about. There was one venture he was on down in the Flats that almost got him thrown into the slammer.

The Flats was a rundown commercial area along the Cuyahoga River, where there were defunct factories. *Cuyahoga* is an Indian name which means "Crooked River." The Cuyahoga covers about ten miles as the crow flies and about twenty-five with all the twists and turns it makes. One of Cleveland's claims to fame is that there is one of every type of Draw Bridge known to man along the Cuyahoga.

Billy Blue Shoes and his cohorts were collecting scrap copper from abandoned factories. They were stripping the copper pipes and electric wires when their torch caught the place on fire. They barely got out before the fire department and cops arrived.

Billy Blue Shoes had taken me to a place in the Flats called Diamond Jim Brady's, which was owned by Rose's father, Jim Vinci. It seemed that he owned a lot of places in Cleveland.

We went in through the back and peered through the kitchen door into the hall. There were cops all over the place in full dress uniform and girls with barely anything on dancing on the tables. Billy Blue Shoes pointed out one table and told me those guys were the Mayor and his people. I got an impression of the person Rose's father might be.

Cleveland was a tough town, and parts of it were downright dangerous. On the weekend, you could look down the main drag, and as far as you could see, there might be three or four cars moving. After dark, even the cops wouldn't go into some sections. St Luke's Hospital was in one of those sections. I was concerned for my safety since I had to go there all times of the day. The X-ray procedures they performed in the ER were for "foreign objects." That's not soft tissue, that's a bullet or knife blade.

I learned Rose's father was having bypass surgery in St. Vincent's Hospital, another one of my customers. The Chief Technologist's name was Clarabelle. She was a nun and a neat kind of person.

Since I was in the place anyway, I stopped by and donated a pint of blood. I knew how much this was needed because my third daughter had several changes of blood due to the Rh factor difference between her mother and me. I was positive, and she was negative.

Billy Blues Shoes told me Rose's father had been given a list of people who had donated blood, and of course, my name was on it. Apparently, Jim was very impressed that a stranger had donated blood in his name. Rose told him who I was.

Anyway, all this led me to wonder that if there was someone who could get me a gun for protection when I had to go to St. Luke's, it would be Jim Vinci, Roses father. I mentioned this to Billy Blue Shoes and got an appointment to meet with Jim in his place in the Flats, Diamond Jim Brady's. He was seated at a table in the middle of the place looking at a small TV when I got there. I explained my concern. He told me he knew nothing about such things, but if I'd give him week, he'd find out what he could. Sure. He didn't know about those kinds of things. When I saw him again the next week, he told me I'd have to apply for a permit and attend a State Police training course. I thanked him for the information, but I was concerned about the trouble I would get into if I had to use the gun, which I didn't as yet have. He told me that if something unfortunate were to happen, I should call him right away, and he'd take care of things for me. I thanked him very much and left that place very impressed—not impressed in a good way, but more impressed with how much I did not want to be indebted to Jim Vinci. I thought about the guy in the Rainbow Room back in Runnemede. I never did get a gun and never saw Jim Vinci again.

Billy Blue Shoes stopped over at my apartment one Saturday afternoon to visit, and he had a friend with him. Billy introduced the guy as Danny. A little later, I went to the kitchen to get us another beer and noticed a big black car in the driveway with someone sitting in the driver's seat. When I asked about that, Danny told me it was his car and there was nothing to worry about. We passed the afternoon talking about darts and other things, and I learned Danny's last name was Green. I wondered if this was *the* Danny

Green? There were a lot of headlines about a supposed war going on between mob factions, and the leader of a faction was named Danny Green. A few weeks later, I asked Billy Blue Shoes if that had been *the* Danny Green in the newspaper he'd brought to my apartment. It was. I asked that he not bring him around again. I joked I was pretty sure the FBI probably had investigated me and my whole family by that time. He told me not to worry, that he hadn't seen Danny lately, that he'd dropped out of sight and could be anywhere. He hoped Danny was somewhere on a sunny beach, but he could be in the trunk of a car in Toledo.

*Guilt by association is something to keep in mind when you are meeting new people.*

I developed and ran a Dart tournament named The Last Annual Everything Handicapped Non-Tournament directed at those players who weren't good enough to win at a regular type of tournament. It was unique in that it wasn't really handicapped due to the manner in which prize money could be won. The entrants seeded themselves into one of three brackets through demonstrating their ability as part of registering for the tournament. They then played an equal number of people from each bracket in qualifying rounds, and the top qualifiers from each bracket played for the prize money for their bracket. I ran this tournament twice before I was transferred back to the East Coast for my job.

I wrote an eight-page pamphlet titled "Beginning the Sport of Darts" and had it printed and sold through the local dart shop during my last years in Cleveland. It was well received.

# The 1980s

# PROMOTED/DEMOTED

By this time my job, relocated me back to the East Coast. I was a Sales Service Supervisor and had an office in Concord Plaza, Wilmington, Delaware, although I lived in Fox Creek, Woodbury, New Jersey.

My job was effectively the same as the sales manager's but I was several pay grades lower.

I studied Peter Drucker's X&Y plus the Japanese Z theories of management. I bought into the Y and Z theories, especially as they applied to field service work. I attended many courses on training and related issues. Time/Territory management, Management by Objective, Defensive driving, Managing Behavioral change, Performance review, Career Development, Impact Expectations, Interdependence and Principles of problem identification, analysis, decision making, and implementation.

My job responsibilities included workload distribution and manpower needs assessment; locating, hiring, and training; performance review and evaluation; ensuring an accident-free performance; effectiveness in territory management; customer relations; new equipment installation and customer training; contract sales; service responsiveness; evaluating and keeping current with market needs changes; and reporting of each of these facets.

## Performance Reviews

In the beginning of my time as a Service Supervisor, a large part of my job was assisting

Sales Service Representatives with the management of their territories. Customer relations were the major component of their mission. The principle product the customers bought was X-ray film. The film was specific to DuPont machines. DuPont had a proprietary system for loading/ unloading cassettes with film, which did not require a darkroom.

SSRs had several ways to enhance the DuPont image in the eyes of their customers. Keeping the equipment running trouble free while helping with exposing and developing high-quality studies were part of that. These contributed to high-volume patient turnover, which contributed to the revenue produced by the Radiology department. Radiology was one of the few profit-producing departments. The management method I chose followed the Peter Drucker Y style of management, where the direct report person was given the responsibilities of running a given geographic territory of customers and the freedom to do that to the particular satisfaction of the customers within that territory. There were fifteen field-based SSRs who covered Ohio; Michigan; Pennsylvania; West Virginia; Virginia; Washington, DC; Maryland; and Southern New Jersey. It just made sense to let the SSR make his/her own schedule of the work needed to be done and to complete that scheduled work.

Time and Territory Management became part of each SSR's skill set. Equipment servicing and customer relations were other skill sets they needed. When these skills were utilized DuPont became a part of the customer's need for high quality and a reason for doing business with DuPont.

I regularly traveled with each SSR and discussed their needs for the job and their plans for professional progression. I made it my business to know what was needed to accomplish my job. We were an integral part of the sales team.

One of my duties was to keep the SSRs fully informed of the activities and changes occurring to the business of being a service person within our region. To that end, I held annual meetings and looked for locations which would be a reward for the SSRs. I chose an upscale hotel in Center City Philadelphia; a ski resort in Western Pennsylvania; an upscale hotel in Annapolis, Maryland; and the Golden Nugget Casino in Atlantic City, New Jersey. The other supervisors held meetings in DuPont office buildings, which caused some jealousy among SSRs.

It was then I learned about promotion potential as part of performance evaluation. Without a college diploma, upward mobility is severely limited, but you are not told of this fact. The whole evaluation of potential is never discussed or revealed when you work below a certain grade in the Salary Assessment system. This SAS is a standard taught in MBA courses and, I think, used by most mega-corporations. Your upward mobility potential is set by your first supervisor and, except for rare instances, will remain as it is no matter what you do. Such was the life of someone without a college diploma and who was seen as a person who worked with their hands.

I justified the location of where I lived through the travel aspect of the job. The territory I was responsible for was Ohio, Michigan, West Virginia, Virginia, Pennsylvania, South New Jersey, Maryland, and Washington DC. I was to travel with each SSR on a regular basis and worked in my Wilmington office when doing expense and sales/service coordination aspects, which required attending sales meetings. I identified and coordinated the activities of SSRs with TRs with an eye toward enhancing the impact they had on customer decisions for using DuPont products. The cost of the equipment and contribution to X-ray sales was justified through recognized impact on X-Ray film sales. To this end, I would ask Radiologists and Radiology Administrators a direct question, "Why do you buy DuPont products." Through this, I could quantify the effect on X-ray film sales that SSRs had.

DuPont had a lock on Daylight equipment because no competitor had a system like it, and the film which could be used in the equipment was made in a specific way which was patented by DuPont.

My education for how these inter-megacorporation competitions worked was enhanced when I learned our competitors were licensed the right to make their film so it would work in our Daylight equipment. We SSRs would be maintaining equipment so customers could run competitors' X-ray film through it. What? The justification I was told was that the competitors were developing daylight systems, so management decided to get some money through leasing the right to our patent to forestall that eventuality.

Let me tell you my experience with such things. Back when I was an Instrument Mechanic at the Repauno Works in Gibbstown, the major product, DMT, was manufactured through what is called a "batch" system. That's where DMT was "cooked," sort of like baking a batch of cupcakes. Rumor had it that a competitor, Amoco, was developing a continuous manufacturing system that would allow them to sell the product at our cost of making it. That would be the end of DuPont's hold on DMT.

There began a top-secret crash program for us to develop a continuous DMT manufacturing process. All the different skills were put on a twenty-four-hour schedule building this pilot plant for continuous DMT manufacture. Being instrumentation people, we were to install the instrumentation that would run the pilot plant. When we got the blueprints for the instrumentation, we very quickly identified this system would not work. It was nonsense. We mentioned this to our supervisor, and very soon, we were told to go ahead with the plans as they were drawn and to remember this was a secret process we were building. Amoco entered into an agreement, which would allow DuPont to use their patented process. One of those systems was built in South Carolina, and the batch system in Gibbstown was scraped. We never did have a continuous system to develop.

*Bluffing* can be a big part of manufacturing by mega-corporations. It is just on a very high level.

Service became separated from Sales in a reorganization effort to get Service to be a profit center rather than a cost to sales. My new Management was fixed on revenue over customer service. They paid lip service to the customer service aspect of the Sales, Service Representative Job title while I was still focused upon the customer relations aspect.

DuPont had a tuition reimbursement program, so I decided I'd go to college and get that missing diploma. I did that cum laude. I began that quest when I was forty-five and still wasn't aware of my promotional prospects. I remained a babe in the woods relative to the thinking of many corporate Managers. I believed that if I did a good job, my Supervisor would recognize it. Naïve me. I soon learned that although they talked a good game, all my supervisors in the new service business were X-type managers.

My supervisor called me into his office on a day and asked me where a particular one of my SSRs was. My reply of "I don't know, but give me a few minutes and I'll tell you" really set him off. I was Y tending toward Z, and he was X tending toward Scrooge.

Through me, my SSRs had learned how to manage their own territories. They were doing so in a manner that had the salespeople aware of the help they were getting from the good relations they had developed with their customers. I needn't be a cop guarding against an SSR sleeping in late or going off fishing or something. I knew what they were about and why. We'd struck a deal during their performance reviews for expectations they set and to which I agreed. They had a stake in the satisfaction of their customers with the performance of their DuPont equipment. They were about meeting or surpassing those expectations. This subtlety and its advantages was lost on X managers.

I was producing more and better results than either of the other supervisors, but it took a couple of years before my supervisor accepted that. In the meantime, my supervisor and his boss, my national manager, had decided I didn't fit in their Region and set about getting me out.

I hired the first female SSR because she was the most qualified applicant. I did it after the pronouncement "There'll never be a female SSR in my region" from my manager. This contributed to my demise as a service supervisor.

I believe they would have fired me on some pretext or other if it weren't for my past acquaintance with the Chemical Industrial Union. They thought I would not go quietly.

In one of my performance reviews, I was told I should report to the office in Clifton, New Jersey, three days per week to learn how to be a service supervisor from the other two service supervisors who worked out of that office. The Clifton office was a two-hour drive, and not even within the geographic territory in which my SSRs worked.

In my last performance review as a Service Supervisor, my manager learned I was producing more income than the other two, and I was doing that through my SSRs selling more Preventative Maintenance contracts than both of them combined. They were making many more service calls than my people were.

I told him I could produce a lot more income from service calls if he wanted. All I'd have to do was stop doing preventive maintenance and have the number of service calls go way up, as the other two had going on in their territories. We'd have to inform the Salespeople we were going to do that since they would have to address the increased dissatisfaction of their customers.

*Being right is not always in your best interest.*

There came a realignment of the Service Region. Medical and Graphic Arts (printing) were combined. The other two

Supervisors and their SSRs had been working that way all along, whereas I had only been in Medical Radiology.

I was demoted from Supervisor but did not have my pay cut. Instead, I went a number of years without a raise.

I think if I were to be fired at that time, my record and length of service would have brought on some questioning. I'll give you some background: DuPont was still a patriarchal-leaning corporation. Awards for length of service were still being presented. The advantages to the corporation of loyal employees were recognized. This was before "Throw away labor" became the fad.

During my time as an SSR, two of the higher-ranked people of Management traveled a couple of days with me in my territory in Ohio. They were assessing the contribution field service could make to the revenue/profit of DuPont. I made a good impression. We talked about my Grandfather and my Father having retired from DuPont and that I was looking forward to doing that. We talked about my three daughters, and since one of the Management people was a woman, I asked if she had some tips I could share with my girls about being a woman in the corporate world. She suggested I bring them to her office in Wilmington, which surprised me. I did that, and after I introduced them, she excused me with, "I'll show them around. Stop back in about an hour." I don't know what went on and when I asked one of my girls today, they don't seem to remember. I feel certain that visit must have made some impression.

Anyway, my name was known in circles much higher than the level of my service management. In any case, I was put in an office without a specific assignment, just some vague instruction that I was to look for opportunities for service people.

Home movies were the up-and-coming thing in home entertainment, and video tapes were just beginning to show up. I was given a lead. I traveled to a part of Wilmington where the street was lined on one side by red brick buildings. I found the rooms I needed and met a group of engineers. I learned that the people who were getting into the home movies business were making copies of video recordings in the batch method. There was a master player which was connected to a gang of slave recorders so there could be a batch of VCR tapes made at once. They had to be made at the speed the master tape was played. On one wall, there was a two-reel recorder/player kind of thing with two reels in place that looked as though it was ready to show me something. This was the machine I was there to ascertain the prospect for service support.

You know how you can watch a Video Tape Player turn and the tape move across the player heads as a movie is being played? The machine on the wall wasn't waiting; it was running. The tape was moving so fast it looked as though it was standing still. That difference in speed was the next big deal in video recording, and I was standing right there, in a top proprietary laboratory, looking at it. I learned that, as with many DuPont products, there was no plan for going to market with the miracle machine. The plan was to finalize the development and then license the technology to the movie makers. There was no servicing opportunity.

I was unacquainted with investing beyond listening to Wall Street reports, but as I walked to my car, the hair on the back of my neck stood up at the information I had, and I just knew there was a terrific opportunity at hand. If only I knew how to take advantage of it. I didn't even know who I should speak to about this.

This opportunity got away because I was ignorant of that aspect of life.

Learn as much about as many things as you are able before you see any use for the knowledge. The Boy Scouts have a motto for this: "Be Prepared."

Soon after this experience, I was put into the manufacturing plant where the Daylight Equipment was made.

I was out of the service business and in the training business.

I was attached to the new Training Center as an equipment specialist on some equipment I'd never seen before, as well as equipment I was an expert with. As such, I was the backup support and contact for field SSRs, when they needed expert advice on a specific problem they were dealing with. I didn't stand a chance of succeeding with that narrow job description.

The training center was built, and I attended the three-week Magar Criterion Referenced Instruction (CRI) course in San Francisco, California. Montessori runs along similar lines. I took on the training mission. I developed a training program for SSRs using the CRI principles.

I began working closely with the engineers to develop the training documentation for customers and SSRs.

I wrote copy-righted computer programs and used a set that not only improved learning but also reduced learning time. It could be used by field Supervisors to confirm the expertise of their SSRs. This reduced the three-week courses to just two weeks.

In one of my performance reviews with my new Supervisor, he couldn't understand how I put up with the treatment I was getting. I still believed that good guys wore white hats and always won.

DuPont was developing a program for collecting silver from fixer fluid in filter-like units connected to X-ray film developer machines called processors, and to collect undeveloped silver from scrap film. DuPont got into silver recovery from scrap X-ray film and developer fixer fluid. It was thought to be less expensive to get money from recovery to offset purchases on the commodities market for manufacturing X-ray film. Plus, it enhanced DuPont's image.

I was assigned to that business.

My job was to buy used X-ray film and help customers who bought DuPont X-ray film comply with RCRA (Resource Conservation and Recovery Act) standards. I studied RCRA compliance requirements and designed and installed DuPont equipment systems to remove silver from the fixer solution in X-ray film processing machines. This put me into the world of precious metal recovery. Talk about suspicious—the people in that business invented the word. They were like high-level junk dealers who wanted to buy a hospital or printing company's trash—but trash that contained precious metal. In this case, silver. The black area on an X-ray film is silver. The fluid in the machines that developed the film contained the silver that was unexposed to X-rays and washed off the film.

# SCRAP FILM BUSINESS

There were businesses, dealers, who recovered these materials from hospitals and printers. The dealers were working to buy at the lowest price possible and sell it to those in the silver-refining business. There were a lot of shenanigans involved in both ends of these deals. When I came into this business, it was at the level where the dealers were selling what they had purchased. I had to overcome the suspicions of these people. After I studied how this business and the transactions were conducted, I had what it took to do that. DuPont, through me, became a force in the silver recovery business.

In order to penetrate the scrap film business I had to gain the confidence and trust of those who were in the business. I had myself and the DuPont expertise to sell. Our process of identifying silver content of scrap film came from manufacturing it, and the method of identifying the value of the scrap film. Thus the amount of money we could pay them was based on science, not gimmicks.

After I earned their trust, and in order to pay them the most we could, I had to learn the way their business worked at the street level. I already knew how it worked from the DuPont level.

New York City. Now there was a different animal for doing business, and I managed to reach a level of trust with the dealers that allowed me to travel with them when they visited hospitals to bid on lots of scrap film about to be released for sale. This alone was no mean feat.

They introduced me as the DuPont Representative they worked with in recovering silver from scrap film. This enhanced their image and allowed them some prestige in this junk man level of commerce. I used the fact that they bid against each other to advantage, by defining the advantage they had over those who did not have DuPont. They could use their superior business sense, combined with my help, identifying silver content in the scrap film, to lessen the chance of overbidding.

One of my trips involved a trip to a hospital in Manhattan with Ned to look over the lot of film to be offered for bid. It went like this: We drove to the hospital through Manhattan, and I learned how that was done in New York style. You see, in South Jersey, when we wanted to change lanes, we'd put on our directional signal to let the other driver know that was what we wanted to do. Then we waited for someone to give us room to make our move. This often took some patience. In Manhattan, with all lanes of traffic filled bumper to bumper, this courtesy kind of thing changed. There you put on your directional signal to tell the other driver you were moving over, not to ask permission. I found out what I had taken for ignorant behavior of not allowing me to change lanes and having to bull my way over with the width of paint between cars, was the only way to break into a line of traffic. Two inches of space was all a taxi needed to break into your line of traffic and allow several more to follow. Putting on your directional signal is being courteous since you were warning the other driver you were moving over, whether they liked it or not.

When we arrived at the hospital, we entered a parking lot. It was a ground-level, open-area parking lot, which is rare, indeed, in Manhattan. As we climbed out of the car, a kid carrying a bucket came over and asked if Ned wanted his car washed. Ned handed him a $5 bill, and we went on our way. "That kid isn't going to wash your car," I said. "My tires won't be slashed either," Ned told me.

The hospitals are all very busy places, what with delivery and repair and other sorts of trucks looking to get a place on the loading docks. There is a dock-master who oversees this crush of traffic. There was a line of trucks, all waiting to get to the dock. They stretched from the dock out onto and down the street a couple of blocks. Ned nodded, shook hands and left a $20 bill behind. Without the help of this person you'd never get in the line.

Most hospitals in Manhattan have been there for a long time. The means to travel from floor to floor, and these places are many floors high and are of older technology. Read: slow. There are elevator operators in each of them, and mobs of people crowding in and getting out on every floor stop. We needed to go below the first floor, which is where the logistics offices are located. With most people wanting floors above the first floor, it took a change of procedure for the elevator operator to go down. And by down I mean sub-sub-sub levels. Ned left another $20 behind. Oh, the operator would take you down all right, but you see, only a couple of elevators went below the ground level, and you'd wait a very long time before you'd see that elevator at your sub-sub-sub level, if ever.

We arrived at the office where Ned got the paperwork he needed. He wasn't permitted to get this through the mail. He had to apply to bid in person. The purchasing agent recognized Ned and was very friendly until I was introduced. It then became very stiff and businesslike. I was informed everything was on the up-and-up in the bidding process. I believed him, of course. This was precious metal commodity and needed to be handled in a certain manner. We were shown to the sub-sub-sub dungeon where the film was stored in barrels, in order for Ned to inspect the lot he was going to bid on.

Travel with another dealer showed me another part of the film recovery business in Manhattan. To ensure there were no shenanigans in the process of picking up and identifying of how much scrap film was being sold, the purchasing agent traveled with the barrels of film. Scrap film was sold by weight, so before the loading could begin, the tare weight of the truck needed to be verified. They did this by weighing the empty truck before and after loading. There was a formula for calculating the tare weight of the barrels.

This dealer had me travel with him in his pickup truck behind the truck that was used to pick up the barrels. When the purchasing agent had the paperwork confirming the truck's weight from the state weigh station, the loading could begin. I stayed behind with the truck while the dealer's workers went with the purchasing agent to get the barrels. As soon as they were out of sight the dealer began pulling lead ingots from the frame of the truck to be loaded and put them into his pickup truck. This dealer was showing me how he cheated the hospital in order to demonstrate for me what a clever businessman he was. The idea that he was showing me that he was a cheat, and not to be trusted, never entered his mind. It was another fact of business in New York City.

The particulars of business in New York weren't the same in Indianapolis, Indiana. Not as much of a crush of traffic and payoffs, but the business tactics were the same. The people were different also. One fine, older gentleman picked me up at the hotel, and over breakfast, we got to know each other personally. As we were walking out, he stopped by the piano in the entranceway and played a few bars of "Back Home Again in Indiana," something we'd spoken of earlier. They had different ways of judging your character in this area.

DuPont's entry into the business of recovery of silver from the fixer liquid in X-ray developer machines (processors) was instigated in part by the opportunity to become involved with their graphic arts customers (printers). I was assigned to that business.

My job was to help our customers comply with the Resource Conservation and Recovery Act (RCRA), covering the amount of silver in the effluent they discharged into the local waste water. This took me into graphic arts companies who had printing plants the size of airplane hangars you see in airports. And waste water purification plants in places that included New York City, Pennsylvania, and Northern Kentucky, which served Cincinnati. These waste water plants had pipes whose size was measured in feet, not inches.

At the time, there were ecology movements such as "Save the Bay" around Baltimore. The hot topic of the time was to reduce pollution in the air and water.

I helped develop a testing system for identifying how much silver was in the discharged effluent, and then design a recovery system to reduce that to within legal limits if needed.

The first step for me was to arrange a meeting with the officers of the business to explain what RCRA had to do with their business. My job was to visit the plants: take samples, send them to laboratories, and return with a plan to address the situation if the discharge was outside of the limits imposed by RCRA.

Whoever wrote RCRA did it the right way. I saw firsthand the effect of the Act on the attitude of the printer company Management people. The normal course of action when confronted with issues such as this was evidenced when, in the course of explaining the compliance requirements, I was asked the likelihood of being visited by an inspector and how much the fines would be if by some chance an inspector arrived at their plant. They wanted to consider whether they should even worry about this, and then if building the cost into the cost of goods and passing that on to their customers was feasible. Then weigh that against the cost of silver recovery.

After I explained the cost could be $25,000 per day of noncompliance levied against the Corporation, *and* $25,000 levied against the person responsible for compliance, they recognized the seriousness of this. There needed to be someone assigned the responsibility for compliance.

I met the person who developed the RCRA manual for DuPont. He and his wife were members of the same church as my wife and me. I saw reduction in the number of inspectors brought on by the cutback on money available for the salaries of inspectors. The response of the people involved in the enforcement of RCRA was to make the penalty money, which came from fines, available for salaries for inspectors.

RCRA came up for reauthorization by Congress, and compliance no longer was a topic of concern of businesses.

Public concern with protection of quality of air and water can be overridden by Congress.

# SINGLE LIFE

When I moved back to New Jersey, my eldest daughter chose to move in with me. I was delighted, and I think in some ways, it pushed her mother's thoughts of me in an equal and opposite direction. I was traveling quite a bit in those years.

There had been an experiment in lawyering in Cleveland, where a group of lawyers tried a law firm on the order of a fast food approach: Reasonable product for reasonable price.

I sued for divorce to get out from under the threat of my soon-to-be ex-wife being able to raise the amount of money I had to send her whenever she felt like it: my sword of Damocles. In the divorce settlement, which was developed from the separation agreement she'd had written up by her lawyer, I had one sentence added. In her rush to get as much money as she could, she and her lawyer failed to read the final paragraph, on the last page, the signature page of the manifold-page divorce agreement.

I had a sentence inserted that said if my ex-wife ever brought this divorce agreement up again, I would automatically assume permanent and total custody of the children. I'd wanted that from the get-go. She agreed to this. I'd coaxed her a bit with 70 % of the proceeds of the sale of the house we jointly owned. When she discovered this, I'm pretty sure her dislike for me was not diminished.

> *What a person pays a lawyer isn't always an indication of the outcome of a dispute.*

Sometime later, my middle daughter decided that she wanted to move in with us. We rented a house in Pitman, New Jersey. Good days.

I had an unfortunate experience with a law enforcement officer. While on a date, I was stopped and arrested for DUI. My lawyer told me to just plead guilty since it only involved a fine. I did and found out his advice was wrong. The judge was going to revoke my driver's license for a year. I choked. Since there was a time period before the ruling took effect, I hired another lawyer and made the decision to move to Chadds Ford, Pennsylvania, just outside of Wilmington, Delaware. That way, I could walk to work if I had to. As it turned out, the result of my DUI hearing was that my initial lawyer was found incompetent and the verdict was thrown out.

With my move from New Jersey, my daughters decided to stay there. They found an apartment in Gibbstown. My youngest daughter married her high school sweetheart and found an apartment in Paulsboro, New Jersey.

Chadds Ford was a totally new area to me. It was rich in history. In one direction was the Brandywine Battlefield and in the other, the Brandywine River Museum. I soon discovered that many great American artists not only displayed their works in the museum but actually had homes in the area. The likes of Howard Pyle, Frank Schoonover, and generations of the Wyeth family are just a few of the great painters known to the area.

I was living the single guy's life and discovered the local watering hole, The Chadds Ford Inn. The people I met were of a different class altogether. Not only did locals frequent there, but you can imagine my surprise when on separate occasions I saw Pavarotti and Brook Shields.

One night I met a guy who introduced himself to me as Frolic. He told me he had been named after the family dog, a foxhound. Frolic was somewhat eccentric but, in the setting of the inn, was amiable. We struck a chord and soon became drinking acquaintances. Much later, I learned his real name was George Weymouth. No wonder we got along. We had something in common. We were both named George. I joked with him and said that if we said his name quickly, the people at the museum across the street might let us in for free, thinking his name was Wyeth.

The Brandywine Museum became another of my favorite places to visit and take dates. On one visit, as I rounded a corner, a painting caught my attention. It was a beautiful field of yellow flowers. I looked at the signature and saw it was George Weymouth. I could have died on the spot. This is one of my most embarrassing moments in life. Frolic was *the* George Weymouth who had painted portraits of Pavarotti and Prince Phillip.

The next time I walked into the inn, I went straight to him and apologized profusely. He responded with laughter so hard he cried. I learned something that day. I'd hit it off with him because he knew I didn't know who he was. This went for most of the people who frequented the inn.

When driving home through Philadelphia, it was often at sundown, and the setting sun was shining on the Philadelphia Art Museum. This became my favorite building. The hue in the reflected sun looked almost golden. I visited that museum a lot. I experienced an awakening, sort of, on one of my visits there. I had some favorite paintings: A little one, about the size of standard paper: 8.5" x 11" because it was oil on wood, and I was fascinated by how small a brush had to be used. Another favorite was *Reclining Nude,* because it struck my humorous side. It was about ten feet by eight feet and was of a gorilla. There was another called *Barn Door*, and it wasn't on the list of paintings on display. You had to ask for it to find it.

I had a date with me and was wandering around in this place showing her my favorites. It didn't hurt in the impression department for a woman to see that side of a guy. We came to the Jan Van Eck painting, and a guard mentioned he noticed we were studying the painting. What studying? We were looking at it. He came to us and pulled out a magnifying glass. Lo and behold, it was a painting of two men looking down on a lake, with people and horses and dogs around it and a gondola and gondolier. As we walked away, I was struck by the realization of how many times I'd looked at that painting and not seen it. I wondered how many other things in my life I'd not seen.

I realized I'd been on the discovery of a different level of appreciation for some time. When I was doing so much driving, I found I was bored with the same songs on the radio. After the third time I heard one of the popular songs, it became boring. I looked for something different and came up with the theme song for the TV show *Victory at Sea*. It told the story of the WWII naval war and did it with the emotions that described the times: From anticipation to participation in violent battles to final victory. My next experience was with "Rhapsody in Blue."

I became a fan of Classical music. I could listen to that over and over, and it never became boring; it just became more fascinating. When I had my daughters in the car with me, I'd play that music. Some of that took.

At this time, I also started to listen to and develop an appreciation for jazz. It's hard to describe. It's a feeling one gets when listening. Trombonist J. J. Johnson once said, "Jazz is restless. It won't stay put, and it never will."

On another trip, I'd gone to Kansas City and sought out the corner of Twelfth Street and Vine so I could stand there like it says in the song. It wasn't much to see: just a corner with a street sign, and there weren't even buildings. The area had been demolished. It was another jazz town. After that, I ended in a place with jazz music. It took some looking to find the place we were in that night. We were at a small table in a kind of balcony. It was another house band with the same songs they'd played a few thousand times. It was okay. I leaned over the rail and shouted: "Do You Know What It Means to Miss New Orleans?" and got a nod and a "Next Set."

The next set came, and they opened up with my request. You know how each person takes a turn with a riff as they play, and each person knows the piece, and each person just plays the notes for their riff without much emotion? Well, as the trombone guy was loosening up his lips and licking them and sliding the slide in and out getting ready for his riff, he snapped his head and looked at the piano player, who was into his riff. Something had happened: the piano player played right through where his riff was to end, and for the next half hour, we got to hear Jazz played the way Jazz people play it for themselves. This kind of spontaneous thing doesn't happen often, but the audience can sometimes bring it on.

You either have it or you don't when it comes to being a Jazz player.

I invited my daughters to the townhouse I was renting for Thanksgiving dinner. I wanted this to be special and was looking forward to their visit. I took great care in preparing squab and vichyssoise. They told me they liked the little chickens but didn't care for the cold potato soup so much.

My life as a chef was over before it had begun.

On an autumn day in Chadds Ford, I was walking in the woods with my new camera, looking to get a picture of something great. I noticed a leaf dangling from a branch that was the prettiest color I'd ever seen. I looked around and saw all the trees were filled with leaves of so many great colors!

How long had this been going on anyway?

Over drinks one afternoon, I announced Chadds Ford was going downhill. I knew that because they let a pizza shop open on Route 202 just up the road, and they let me move in. I was prophetic. Soon after that I noticed the plaid-clad middle-management types had begun moving into the newest houses, beginning to populate the area. No more people like Frolic or the others. They disappeared to some other place, and I started looking for a house. The prices in Chadds Ford pushed me to move away too.

I bought a house in Wilmington and set about decorating it, which showed my lack of taste in decorating.

Brown curtains held together with safety pins would not make it into the pages of *House Beautiful* or *Better Homes and Gardens*.

# NEW ORLEANS ADVENTURE

There came a cry for help from the TR for one of the largest hospital customers we had in the South, the Ochsner Foundation Hospital; and I, being the expert, was told to see what I could do. This was a trip to New Orleans, which was legitimately on DuPont!

I met the Quality Assurance Coordinator. Her name was Sandie. While she showed me around the department and reviewed her complaints, I couldn't help but follow the swing in her get along. I found her very attractive. I identified the problem was not the equipment—it was educating the technologists, and I suggested I hold a training session for them. We agreed that a training session for the techs was called for.

Sexual harassment was the big deal of the day, and a person would lose his job if just a whisper of that were to come up. I was a single guy, and Sandie, the Quality Assurance Coordinator, looking as good as she looked, brought an interest and question to my mind. How could I get to know her on a personal basis, and what could be wrong that had her single? I was very attracted to her, but how to approach this situation made me very cautious. There weren't many women like her around—with character, smarts, and looks—so I worried at this a bit. If she took anything I said the wrong way, I could lose my job.

After I got back to my office, I called her, and I asked for the correct spelling of her last name. I knew what it was, but I wanted an excuse to talk to her. I really wanted to see if I might be able to break the ice toward a more personal relationship. I later learned she saw right through that ploy. To probe for reaction, I mentioned I'd heard New Orleans was a great place to visit and that I was interested in visiting the sights. She said she'd be happy to show me around. Happy day—I made it past the first obstacle.

At the end of the call, we'd set up the training for a Friday, and my flight home wasn't until Sunday, so she could show me around New Orleans on Saturday. Sneaky, I know, but a fella does what he can. This was all going pretty well, and Mr. and Ms. Use (the cutouts I'd made for the training class) were coming in handy.

On my trip to do the training, my second visit to New Orleans, I strolled around the French Quarter alone and stumbled across a trombone case hanging out over the sidewalk. I stopped and looked at the building it was hanging from and discovered this was Preservation Hall. That's *the* Preservation Hall! I returned for the first session of the day early that evening. It cost $2 to get in. It was an old house, worn and dingy. There were a couple of benches, an overstuffed living room chair, a few folding chairs, and various others types of seating, all decrepit. The performers, all five of them, wandered in and milled around on the small stage. Their instruments looked as though they'd fallen off a truck, all bent and dull. All but one of those people looked just like their instruments. Then they started playing.

I was in the Preservation Hall, for sure. How they could play? The show ended, and the few of us who were in there headed for the door. I stopped at the glass case by the door and checked the time of the next performance, paid my next $2, and hung around to kill the hour and a half. There were paintings on the walls. They were dark things of hard-life-looking musicians. I asked if they were for sale. Yes, they were, she supposed, but no one ever asked. But she'd find out. The musicians showed up right at show time and were surprised to see me still there. At the end of that show, the final of the day, I learned the painting I'd been asking about was for sale for $6,000. I could have gotten it for a whole lot less than that, I was sure. Only thing was I didn't know how I was going to get it home on the airplane. I wasn't very worldly. I didn't buy it. What would that be worth today?

On the scheduled day and time, I arrived at the hospital and did the training for the techs, after which Sandie offered to pick me up the next day at my hotel to show me around. I found a place and bought some flowers to break the ice toward a more personal relationship if the right time arose. The dilemma was *how* and *when* and *if* to give them to her and take the risk. After all, I didn't know her, and this could be just another of those bust kinds of dates I'd been having for a few years. I decided to leave the flowers in my room and see how things went. Although it wasn't really a date—it was her being a good host to a visitor to her city. Those flowers could change this relationship, so I had to be very careful. After all, she had to have some guy in her life. I mean, just look at her, for heaven's sake. She arrived right at the time she said she would—wow, a punctual woman!

We walked around the Quarter and stopped at Café DuMonde for hot chocolate and beignets. While there, we decided on a ride on the President, a paddle wheel boat where you can see the sights of New Orleans from the Mississippi River. It was going pretty well although I misjudged the temperature on the River and was freezing cold during the ride.

I learned her personal situation: She was divorced, had someone she was sort of seeing, had her own home, and worked two jobs. At this point, I didn't see a lot of risk with pushing a bit. We were going to Audubon Park Zoo and eating a muffaletta sandwich we'd bought for lunch. The muffaletta is New Orleans' best-known Italian sandwich. I didn't know it had olives in it (I don't like olives—another little sacrifice it took to move the relationship along). I asked if I could go to my room to get a jacket, and she said she needed to use the ladies' room while we were there. The flowers I'd gotten for her were in the room, and there would be no way of keeping her from seeing them. It would have been most embarrassing if I hadn't already decided I wanted to take the risk that she would accept them for what they were: a not-so-subtle way to let her know I was interested. Even so, it was still a bit embarrassing when we entered the room and the flowers were there.

I visited New Orleans again, this time on a personal trip. Sandie visited me at my house in Wilmington. I'd bought a house by then, in 1987. On her second visit to Wilmington, during the ride from the Philadelphia airport, I asked if she would be my wife. She accepted, and we've been a married couple since February 1988.

That year, 1988, was a turnaround year. I got married, graduated from college, and turned fifty.

One of the many contributions Sandie brought to our marriage was combining our finances. When I bought my, which became our, house, I'd gotten a variable rate mortgage that lowered the payments for the first few years. The plan I developed considered that annual increases in salary I would be getting would cover the rising cost of the mortgage. The result of not getting raises meant I was going to lose the house. When we married and shared ownership of all that we had, we refinanced and got a fixed-rate mortgage, which was more affordable.

# DARTS: ON THE SHELF

After returning to New Jersey, I returned to my old haunts and the South Jersey English Dart Association. I joined the team of the Paulsboro Hotel and placed first in all the categories there were the year before I moved to Wilmington, Delaware.

In Delaware, I joined a few teams and became president of the First State Dart League. Darts was a dying activity in Delaware, and I left the sport in 1984 due to lack of competition, being remote from South Jersey and Philadelphia, and my hectic travel schedule.

# The 1990s

# DOWNSIZED

In '93, I was downsized out of DuPont.

Taxes are not set up to help you if you're not in the right tax bracket and don't have lots of deductions. Between the vacation time I had accrued and the incentive pay I was given, I ended up paying as much in taxes as I had gotten in gross income in my last full year of employment.

Not having a job to do is an odd feeling. Adjustment comes slowly.

I was standing in our dining room, sipping from a cup of tea and looking out at the driveway, which was covered with snow two feet deep: *I need to get that cleared off— sometime.* A smile crossed my face. I really didn't have to do that until I felt like it. I felt one of the joys of retirement.

I had a back operation and liked it so much I had another one in '94, which put me on rehab for a good bit of time. During recovery, I had time to think about what I was going to do for a job.

*If you're contemplating retirement you need to get ready
for it with more than money*

We became entrepreneurs.

# AN ALLIGATOR ARRIVED IN WILMINGTON

∞

In New Orleans and the South, there is a confection called a Snoball, which is finely shaved ice soaked with flavoring. The flavors keep up with the reputation New Orleans has for great food. Sandie had been saying ever since she tasted water ice that what Wilmington needed was a Snoball shop. We found ourselves in a situation where I had nothing to do and she was ready to quit work in the medical field. We had some money left from being downsized out of DuPont, so why not?

We'd become small business entrepreneurs.

We bought a market survey, got help from a group of retired people from corporations like DuPont (S.C.O.R.E.) to teach us how to set up the financial tools we'd need. Since I'd already run a business for DuPont, I had a handle on that part of things.

We found a place in New Orleans to get the machines and flavorings. We found places in Wilmington to buy freezers and refrigerators and all the equipment and utensils we needed. I could make the counters and do the plumbing.

The next steps were to find a location, get a name, find a supplier for consumables, and learn how to run a business. How hard could this be?

Finding a location was difficult, and we looked for a few months before we found a place that would be suitable. At least suitable as far as we understood what suitable was. There was a local sandwich shop, very popular, both on a corner of a main street and up against a neighborhood—just what we needed. The sandwich shop took up the front half of the building, and the back part was vacant. It had a basement where we could make the simple syrup (Swamp Water, we called it). Our landlord let us make the alterations we needed, such as pipes from the basement up to the shop and drains down from the mixing stations.

Through Sandie's contacts in New Orleans, we had an artist draw up a logo of an alligator under a lamppost for us. The name was easy: N'awlins Snoballs.

There were four parking places in front of the two large windows in our part of the building and two by the sandwich shop. We figured that since the sandwich shop and our place were carry-out businesses, there were enough parking spaces at the building and along the street. We didn't think about parking being a problem.

My sister came up from Florida for a few weeks, and Sandie's Mom came up from New Orleans for another few weeks, to help us get started. I only saw my children the few times they visited the store. We advertised for help and hired a few high school kids. We learned that the kids who showed up on their own were the ones to hire. We opened our new seasonal business, and it took off. The first year, we were getting busier every week. The money was enough, barely, to cover twelve month's rent from an eight-month season.

Getting help was not a problem; word spread fast among the high school population. In order to help customers pick flavors from the twenty or so we had, each employee had to know the taste of all the flavors, so part of the job was to eat Snoballs.

Our busy hours fit into the times the kids had available, and in the months they had the least school, we had a promotion scheme that let the kids earn more money and have job titles that they liked. We'd wait when parents were late picking up their children, which put us in good stead.

Sandie handled the bulk of the work. The success of the business was mostly because of her fantastic energy and skill with food in general and how quickly she developed relationships with customers. I was a glorified bookkeeper and Snoball maker and pipefitter/repair person.

We both felt the physical pain in the bottom of our feet from standing in one place. For a good part of the day, I was grinding my teeth from the pain in my feet and from my back.

Parking was getting to be a problem. The sandwich shop employees were using the spaces in front of our shop, which left us with none. A conversation with the owner of the sandwich shop and our landlord did nothing to alleviate the problem.

# BUSINESS BECAME FAMILY

Then in '97, I had a heart attack: I worked for it, earned it, and deserved it.

Between N'awlins Snoballs and the hospital, there was no other activity.

I had a vague goal in mind for where we were taking the business, but we had not decided on a goal or the type of business this was going to be before we jumped in.

We were ignorant of these things, and the people from S.C.O.R.E. only told us about the financials involved. It wasn't their fault since they only had experience in the megacorporation world and didn't know about the grind of a Mom-and-Pop operation. They thought sitting behind a desk and analyzing numbers in a spreadsheet was the most important part of a business.

The best thing for us would have been to decide whether we wanted a plan to take our business to an absentee management–type business or to have it be like the sandwich shop, which was a hands-on family business.

If they were lucky, after-hours doing the business then the spreadsheet was part of the job.

We had no plan for when we would retire from making Snoballs or switch to just managing the business or franchising or whatever we would do with the business. We were just trying to get it to produce a good income.

A good business plan should include the direction the business is to take over the long term. And include contingencies for negative things that may be anticipated to happen, as well as for how wild success will be handled. We had neither.

As we were closing one night, toward the end of our second year, a car crashed through the entrance of our shop and missed crushing Sandie by seconds. During the time we were closed, we looked at our financials and customer comments and made the decision to step up our business from a seasonal one to a year-round operation. We had outgrown this location. We found a new location about a mile from where we were. Finding a location for a microbusiness is very hard.

There was a small strip mall on a heavily traveled street bordered by two large neighborhoods. A developer had just bought the place and was looking to bring it to life with us and a bar/pool hall, added to the three other businesses which had been there for years.

The developer had history with a local politician, as did all the developers in the area.

# THE ALLIGATOR GETS KILLED

It happened that the developer was doing business as he always had, cutting a corner or two, which put him at odds with Bob the politician, the politician/lawyer, who had written the new Land Use Law. Bob the politician wanted to punish the developer. He attended civic association meetings and whipped up angst over what was happening to their neighborhood. He used an approach right out of the stage show/movie *Music Man.* There was to be a pool hall "right here in Fairfax and Deerhurst."

When the owner of the pool hall applied for his liquor license, there were busloads of people there to protest. One of the people who lived right across the street from our shop came in to look our place over. He told me we had a nice kind of place, but he wouldn't let his children come because there was to be a pool hall next door. *What?*

We were to open the new location the week after July 4th. We had to move the shop over the three-day weekend. As the time to move came closer, we were inspected by the fire department and the health department. We thought we were ready. Who ever heard of a Certificate of Operation (CO): Everyone but us apparently.

*It pays to consult local politicians before making any decision concerning a business.*

It is necessary to understand the nature of the common politician. They may appear to be nice, concerned people; but remember what they did, or have to continue to do, in order to get and keep their livelihood, which is how many of them view the office they hold. They are not public servants, as we are told they are—they are businesspeople whose business is to get voters to believe they have the people's best interest at heart when that is, a lot of the time, the case after their own best interest is served: *that* comes first. Remember Maslow and his hierarchy of needs?

An official from the Land Use Department showed up at our shop and informed us we could not open for lack of a CO. Our landlord accepted the blame for this and sent me, along with one of his partners, to the Land Use Department to get the needed CO. We weren't able to get it because we were in violation of the Land Use Law: there weren't enough parking spaces. There were many more than the four we had at the other location. The guy at the Land Use Department was apologetic, and it was evident he was following orders. Bob the politician was involved. We had to get a variance from the parking conditions established by the new Land Use law. This had to be sought from the Land Use Board.

Our lawyer received a one-page notice that the variance wasn't in compliance with the new Land Use Regulations. When I went to my lawyer's office a few days later, there were four-foot-high piles of paper that pled our case. We were up against a really nasty person. He was trying to get the developer and using us to do it. So we applied for a variance, prepared for our case being heard and off to Land Use Variance hearing we go. Customers, employees and their parents also showed up. We won and went on with our business for a few years.

The year 2000 rolled around, and since I could begin collecting Social Security and we had a comfortable business going with what appeared to be a good future, we thought to look into selling N'awlins Snoballs. We asked our developer if he could sell it. He said, of course, and within a week, there were three enquiries. One was looking good and at the price we were asking. The prospect wanted to see all the paperwork, of course. He asked about the variance. I called the Land Use people to get something from them that said the variance was solid. I was told the people at County Land Use would have to get back to me on this, and Red flags went up: Bob the politician? The answer that came back was that a new owner would have to get another variance since the one we had was granted to my wife and me personally, not to N'awlins Snoballs. We read through the variance very carefully, and nowhere did our names appear. Bob the politician was up to his tricks again.

Interest in buying N'awlins Snoballs went the way of the proverbial Snoball in Hades.

We looked up lawyers who had experience in this field and called the most prominent one. She told me that after checking with Bob the politician, she could take the case. *What?* She asked him if she could take our case? We checked another lawyer and learned there would be a $10,000 retainer fee with no guarantee of success. Bob the politician had made it so we couldn't build any equity in our business and couldn't sell it. After the years we'd been forced to fight Bob the politician, now we find he'd thrown up another roadblock, a very expensive one. Our dream was crushed. We sold the name and equipment for cents on the dollar to someone out of State and retained just enough money to pay off the mortgage on our home.

Hollywood is fond of producing movies where a downtrodden person who was being taken advantage of by mean-spirited politicians triumphs, proving you can beat town hall. No, you can't. That's a myth. Guys like Bob the politician can bleed you dry of money one piece of paper at a time.

# RETIREMENT

My wife and I tried a traditional retirement kind of life: we took what we called tooling trips. We visited my mother and my sister in Florida, then my in-laws in Louisiana and Mississippi, and friends in Georgia and Ohio.

This kind of life's attraction wore off a bit, especially for my wife. She needed things to do, but not so much for me.

My mother and my sister lived in Florida, and I only got to see them a couple of times a year. When my mother reached the point where she could no longer live alone, my sister, who had been working at being her caregiver for many years, needed to fill me in on that situation. I tried to handle her business from Delaware but found it difficult. I moved her up to Wilmington and took over the role of caregiver. This was a very time-consuming task, but it was made easier if you applied the old saw "He ain't heavy, he's my brother" for whomever you are helping. We made the last years of my mother's life as comfortable for her as we could make it.

Being a caregiver is a role that comes unexpectedly.

# The 2000s

# FAMILY

Everyone can draw, so said the instructor of my art class at Neumann College. To prove a point, she asked each of us to draw a house and a horse. We did, with the predictable results we all know: a not-so-square house with crooked windows and an animal recognizable only because it had a leg on each corner and a head on one end. We all had a chuckle at what we'd produced and took that as proof that we could not draw. Our instructor blamed our third-grade drawing ability on spelling and arithmetic. This is where I learned the role of the hemispheres of my brain. We'd all drawn what the left side of our brain knew as a house and a horse. They were the first ones we'd ever drawn that were stored in the left side of our brain and were the ones brought up to use. We were going to learn how to draw what we were seeing rather than what we had stored in the left side of our brain; we were going to learn to use the right side of our brain, hence the class text "drawing from the right side." Anyway, the reason for our inability to get in touch with the right side of our brain, according to our instructor, was that we started using the left side for rote memorization of characters and numbers and discontinued use of our right side for creative thinking.

I decided I needed a worktable to use for my art class work, and since I had some tools from my father's house, and having some knowledge in using them, I set out to build one. It turned out to be more of a contraption and not all that sturdy on its legs, but it did the trick. This was my first venture into furniture/cabinet building.

I decided I needed a pantry. I built it in the basement. This I built with recessed doors that required a router, so I bought one. This came out pretty well, except for the wood I chose, which was inexpensive white pine. As it dried, it warped. Not a good thing.

The mantle for the fireplace in our living room and my discovery of exotic hardwoods came much later on. The beauty and the depth of the grains and the colors fascinated me. I wanted to use them, so I began looking for projects. Keepsake boxes—you know the little boxes people put things in to keep but no one really uses anymore—became a project. I was inspired by a little inlay my dad had made that I managed to have through the good graces of my stepmother's daughter.

I need to explain that remark.

The home once shared by my dad and my stepmother had originally belonged to my grandparents. When my stepmother moved into a home for the aged, her daughter took over her affairs. I was invited over to go through my dad's workshop and take what I wanted.

My dad had passed away a few years earlier after a heart attack and a bypass procedure failed him.

The surgeon who did the bypass went on vacation right after the operation and left the recovery part of things to the hospital staff. In any case, the surgeon wasn't around, and no one was monitoring my dad's decline, putting pressure on his weakened heart. It couldn't handle it after having to endure a second procedure, which had been required to fix a problem left from, or caused by, the first procedure. I believe my dad died because of that. I wanted to pursue that, but my stepmother said no.

*Don't trust hospital staff to do what is supposed to be done. Ask questions, get answers, and get proper care.*

So this is how I came to be invited to the house that my dad had told me he left to me in his will. He explained how those things from my grandfather and my mother and him that he thought my sister and I should have were spelled out in the joint will he and my stepmother had drawn up. He wanted me to know this and what to do when the time came. I was the executor of his will. He and my stepmother had wills drawn up together to identify how their estates would be divided, which is what many people do while making these kinds of plans and wills.

He died knowing his two children would share in what his side of our family left behind.

What he didn't plan for was that upon his death, his widow would assume ownership of everything they had jointly owned; and the day after he died, she changed her will so everything would be left to her daughter, who was then the executrix of her will.

Her daughter lived in California and had no use for the house and the belongings in it. When her mother no longer needed the house, she wanted to unload everything that wasn't worth anything. That included the tools and machines in my father's workshop.

The lesson I learned is that the surviving member of a marriage may, and probably will, have a change of heart concerning the family members of their former spouse relative to what is to be bequeathed.

Anything a person wishes their survivors to have should be given to their survivors prior to their own death. A simple declarative note stating the objects belong to the survivor but is/are being held and used by the person writing the note until their death, will do the trick.

> *If a person is not having positive impact on my life, I do not want them in my life.*

Sandie found a full-time job in retail that she liked very much and soon became recognized as the top performer among her peers.

*A vocation which suits you allows you satisfaction and recognition.*

Darts had not been part of my life since 1984, except for my scrapbook, and I didn't even know where that was.

In preparation for my middle daughter's marriage, we had a get-together for the families at our house. We had the room. Her fiancé' was from Gibbstown, and her future father-in-law had worked with me at the DuPont plant there. They knew of me and my darts exploits, Sandie hadn't a clue. I hadn't brought it up. I was asked if I was still playing, and with that, I poked around in a cabinet and found my scrapbook to bring them up-to-date. Sandie peered over our shoulders as I was showing them my scrapbook, and she exclaimed "You were a world champion? And you didn't tell me?" World champion wasn't exactly correct; "one of the top five in America" was more accurate, although I'd won tournaments where players from around the world participated. That was a detail to me.

At the time I was playing heavily, darts in America was a barroom game like shuffleboard. There were leagues with teams, but few kept records from year to year or statistics. Oh, there were banquets held at season end with averages and team standings and such, but there was no real record keeping. The world of darts had grown significantly while I was not paying attention. It now was a worldwide sport. It had changed from being a game to a sport due to activity in England, where it was the number 3 sport.

After I retired from working for a living, Sandie talked me into returning to darts, where I discovered I had to relearn the things I had previously done innately.

I expanded *Beginning the Sport of Darts* to *Mastering the Sport of Darts*, a twenty-four-page book. I contacted a friend of mine who publishes the preeminent magazine in North America for darts people, *Bulls-Eye News*, and asked if he'd be interested in selling my book. He was, and did.

A couple of years later, I received a phone call from a publisher. He had written *To the Point: The Story of Darts in America.*

He told me he was interested in publishing my book. I waited for the other shoe to drop with the news of how much this was going to cost. It didn't, and I set about writing some additions to make *Mastering the Sport of Darts* into a book with at least the fifty-one pages that he told me was needed.

I began looking for information that would be of interest, not filler kinds of things.

I thought about how the accomplishments of people I knew became stuff of lore and hyperbole and didn't want that to be anyone's legacy. I wanted to add interviews with my compatriots so their stories would not get lost over time.

The introduction of this idea with my compatriots went like this: "I'm going to write a book and I'd like you to be in it."

"Sure you are."

"Yeah, I am, and you should be in it."

"I don't think so. Want a drink?"

"No, think about it: twenty years from now, when we're not around anymore, some kid in Iowa will read what you have to say about darts and what you've done. It'll be what you say, not some stories other people made up."

I wrote my book, and in 2004, *How to Master the Sport of Darts* was released, which was the premier book on the subject in North America. It sold for about $15. Later, when I no longer had any copies and it was out of print, copies sold for well over $100. *What?*

Also in 2004, the Professional Darts Corporation—based in England—known as the PDC, put on a tournament in Boston, Massachusetts, with a bonus prize of $1 million if an American were to win the tournament. That's how confident the promoters were that an American would not win.

I got to thinking: if a whole lot of people watched this event in Boston and became interested in the game of darts, where could such people go to get information about how and where to become involved? The answer was, there was no place to do that. The websites that existed were about individual leagues, not general information.

In 2007, I started Flight School, an online e-mail how-to for darts with an eye toward helping people get more enjoyment through a higher skill level.

I put together a website (www.howtodarts.com) with information about dart leagues, the people who were in the leagues, the different types of tournaments that were being played, various bits of memorabilia, my books, playing record, various articles, Flight School and recorded interviews.

Using some information I was getting from darts people around the world, I wrote *DARTS: Beginning to End* in 2009, which has been a best seller since the day it was released.

Today, I'm the only one gathering information this way, to my knowledge.

Flight School, along with *DARTS: Beginning to End*, is recognized as the best method for perfecting a person's dart game to "as good as can be," and I am in the business of teaching/coaching darts.

# The 2010s

# VOCATION

When I was downsized out of DuPont, I met with a financial consultant, who worked for an investment firm, and rolled over my 401(k) into an investment account.

Until 2010, I visited with him occasionally but mainly just talked since my blue-collar view of things interested him. I didn't make any substantial changes, just bought and sold the low-performing investments. I was becoming more aware of what was going on in the stock market, but only in passing fashion. I became uncomfortable with the way the market in general was behaving. I had no real basis for my discomfort and no expertise; it was just there. I called and told him to sell everything and put me in cash. He wasn't supportive but did what I asked. When the bottom fell out of the market in late August to early September, I had avoided the mass losses that most everyone else, including my sister, suffered. This raised his curiosity concerning how I knew enough to get out early.

I learned something about what financial advisors do.

I started drawing from my account, and after that, I didn't pay any more attention to my account than I did when it was a DuPont retirement benefit, and that was very little.

The year I gave serious thought to retirement was brought on by qualifying for Social Security and selling N'awlins Snoballs. The money we could regularly draw from my retirement account, combined with my pension and Social Security, gave us enough income to allow us to retire. Sandie's income was a bonus that we could use for improving quality of life. We weren't going to live in luxury but we could pay the bills since we'd used money left from selling N'awlins Snoballs and the downsized bonus from DuPont to pay off the mortgage on our home. I protracted the balance of my retirement account out to ten years before it would be used up and we could begin drawing from Sandie's.

> *Looking ahead, far ahead, at debt, bills, and sources of income must be done at least twenty years before you think you may want to, or need to, retire.*

The electric bill came in August of 2010, and I almost choked. I was sitting on our deck, which I designed and we built, Sandie right alongside of me, thinking about what this kind of increase in cost of living would be doing to the plans for how long my money was going to last. There sat our house, our home, and we owned it—no mortgage since we'd gone for security rather than speculative investment. A home with fourteen-inch-thick stone walls, and well insulated. I looked at it as though it were a piggy bank full of money and wondered how I could get that money. I was gratified that we had not been what I term "real estate social climbers," where we kept buying newer, bigger, better houses to live in, refinancing over and over as long as we could.

> *A secure feeling is a good thing and owning your home provides some of that.*

I was considering a list of things we wanted to do to the house to reduce the upkeep and work it required, and this line of thought took me to thinking about how I might increase our cash flow by reducing the cost of heating and cooling the house. That took me to my friend Chris. I met him when we opened N'awlins Snoballs, and he was just beginning his HAVC business. We crawled around on the floor together installing the ice block machines. I asked him to look our house over with an eye to cutting our monthly cost. Solar was the new thing, and I did some research and contacted a solar company to discuss the possibility.

We explored the options we had between oil/gas furnace, electric, and geothermal.

We decided the best, least expensive, course would be geothermal.

The guy came to drill the hole for the pipe, which would be the heat transfer pipe filled with refrigerant for our air-conditioning. The hole had to be one hundred to two hundred feet deep. The drilling rig looked like a city fire truck, it was so big. After three days of drilling, at about 150 feet down, the drill broke through a ceiling over an underground river that was flowing at around two hundred gallons per minute. Since the pipe that would circulate our coolant medium had to be in solid ground, the idea of going geothermal was dead.

Well digging/drilling is a risky business. Unusable hole: no money.

In the end, we went with solar and all electric. It took all the money I had in my retirement account. I'd calculated the heating and cooling cost reduction would cover the loss of income from that account, if all went well. We were insulated from the continuing increasing cost of home-heating oil. I was broke. My calculations had to be right. It has gone better than well. I felt good when Sandie said, "You really did well with what we did."

The drawback to solar is snow. It piles on the solar panels so needs to be cleaned off. And in periods of cold nights and above-freezing days, where ice forms on the panels, it is difficult keep the panels clear.

My job became keeping track of the money coming in from our various sources and going out to support the rest of the world.

Selecting the method to use for heating/cooling your home needs to be done with care.

# CHANGING TIMES

"Like a kid in a candy store" is a good way to describe me in a place that sells exotic hardwoods such as black walnut claro, bloodwood, chestnut, cherry, babinga, mahogany, maple, oak, and such.

I wanted to make something beautiful.

Inspired by a small inlay my father had made I recovered along with his tools, I made a bunch of keepsake boxes while not having any use for what I was making. I marked each with the date, and that it was by me, and then gave one to each of my daughters and my grandchildren. That way, the keepsake boxes became keepsakes. I tried creating a market for them through placing them at a local farmer's market. Nothing. Nada. No one was buying. This went the way of the jewelry I made so many years before.

So much for creating what I call un-necessary items, since I found no market for them. I have a pet name for shops that sell such things: un-necessary shops. These are the places where folks with more money than they need, or less sense than they should have, or who have a compulsion for decoration, spend money. They're not bad places, just not necessary.

A babinga mantle for our fireplace came next: gorgeous thing it is. It was the first real test for cutting a true forty-five-degree cross cut so it made a true ninety degree corner with a tight match across the full length of the corner.

I learned the importance of "leave the line on" and true ninety-degree cuts and the precision it takes to make furniture.

I learned how to set up my tools to make true cuts with less than the width of a pencil-line variance across the entire cut with a perfectly vertical edge on the piece. I spent a good deal of time setting my radial, table, and band saws to make true cuts.

We redecorated one of our bathrooms, and I decided to make the vanity. There was a lot of reserve from Sandie concerning my skill at cabinetmaking, but being the great wife she is, she let me go ahead. I went with mahogany. I learned the difficulty of matching grains and in setting drawer fronts. It looks as good as a store-bought one, only it is much prettier.

The day came when I knew my skill was at a high level. Sandie came to me with a picture of a vanity she'd found and asked if I could make one like it. Wow, she trusted me to make that? How good does that feel?

We selected a South American babinga: very pricy. You've heard of "measure twice and cut once"? Think "measure four times, wait a day, measure again, then cut." It is a show stopper in our other, remodeled, bathroom, with a matching mirror frame on the door of the medicine cabinet.

My daughter asked me if I could make a mantle for her house, and we set about doing that. Visits to the local lumberyard that sold exotic hardwoods and her selecting the wood came first. She showed she's her father's daughter. She chose bloodwood—very rare and costly. No mistakes allowed when cutting this wood. You get one shot at it.

The fireplace and the mantle set the mood for the entire place: just beautiful.

It takes too much to make vanities or to do this kind of work to be a vocation. One of the major drawbacks is controlling the noise and dust. Another is selling them.

There is a market for high-priced handmade furniture, but not for a part-timer.

My life as a furniture maker came to an end.

Sandie continues working her retail job as the best employee among her peers, which I do not find surprising. We use the money she brings in to improve our home and lifestyle.

Sandie has been my partner, as in building the deck twenty-five years ago, but our roles have begun changing. I have become her partner in shoveling snow, mowing the lawn, and doing all the other work needed to keep up our home. She does about all the work and watches over me with "You shouldn't go out without something on your head," or peeking into the living room at me on the couch: "You all right in here? Have everything you need?"

I walked into a place called Pizza by Elizabeth's. It's a nice upscale restaurant we like to go to once in a while. I noticed my brother-in-law and my sister-in-law sitting at the bar. That seemed odd, but since my brother in-law was visiting for a couple of days, not really out of place. It wasn't out of place until I looked beyond them and saw hands waving in the air, a bunch of hands. When I looked more closely, I saw my children, grandchildren, and great-grandchildren were there. It was a surprise birthday party for me. Actually, it was another surprise birthday party since my wife had pulled this on me before. She can be so sneaky when she wants to be.

I was shown to the head of the table and greeted by everyone. As I looked along that table, I noticed how many people were there. There were nineteen of them. When did this all come about?

We didn't gather all in one place except for this kind of birthday surprise. We used to get together as a group on Christmas Eve as a legacy from the separation/divorce. Gathering like this was a compromise reached where I could be with all my children at least once a year. All the other holidays were reserved for their mother. Some compromise!

I don't know of manuals for being a grandfather and great-grandfather, so I'll just wing it.

I have another life tenet: I refuse to put my children in a position to choose between their mother and me. I drop out first.

Over the years, getting together on Christmas Eve has become more difficult. All three girls now have husbands and in-laws with whom they need to spend time. They have children of their own they want to have their Christmas with. So little by little, I've surrendered my claim on Christmas Eve; now it barely exists.

When a son gets married, you tend to gain a daughter; when a daughter gets married, you tend to lose a daughter.

# DARTS: GIVING BACK

I went back to Steel Tip darts in my old stomping ground, Mt. Royal, New Jersey, got onto the Dark Horse Tavern team of the Old English Dart League of Philadelphia, played on Stony's team in the First State Dart League in Delaware (Steel Tip), and joined a team in the National Darts Association (Soft Tip) League in Delaware.

I was invited to attend the National Darts Hall of Fame inductions ceremonies and tournament. I had been selected to be entered into the Hall. Sandie and I attended. It meant a return visit to Clarksburg, West Virginia. It brought back memories of my days in the air force; but this time, I was being recognized, not learning about moonshiners.

I've found that my passion for the game of darts, at least the competing part, has diminished to the point where I no longer compete. I still enjoy my role as a recognized world authority on becoming as good as can be in the sport. Every day I'm involved in an activity that provides me job satisfaction through helping people get more enjoyment from having darts as a part of their life. Opening my e-mail has an uncertain anticipation. I am constantly amazed at some of the countries where my e-mail originates: Thailand, Turkey, Bosnia, several countries on the continent of Africa, and the UK. The commonality and love of the sport joins us all together.

My darts life now consists mainly of my Flight School online darts training program. It's a worldwide venture along with books and website that I run from my den. I occasionally attend tournaments to gather more interviews and keep up-to-date on the ranking leaders. I work daily at trying to bring my avocation into a profit-making vocation.

> *There is much satisfaction from being a mentor/ instructor/supporter.*

# ARTS: FORTITUDE, HEART, OPPORTUNITY

∞

Sport offers unique opportunities for an individual to experience the "thrill of victory and the agony of defeat" even when the level of prowess is neophyte. From the youngest to the oldest among us, that special feeling of preparing for the competition and competing provides a good and necessary addition to our lives, even at the amateur level.

Everyone who participates in any sport, no matter how serious the commitment, is limited by their abilities. Those with significant limitations need the sport to be modified in some manner in order to participate equally, most of the time. But there is a sporting endeavor that is not like that.

People with physical limitations join the legions of amateurs who are devoted to this sport, and follow its own bit of professional activity, because they learn there is also something more, something special about it. And that something special is that they are not so outstandingly different that they require special consideration. That sport is darts.

The struggle to be as good as can be is impressive enough when observed in general, but in darts, the heart exhibited by those with physical limitations gets barely noticed during play of the game. Spectators have their eyes glued to the dartboard as they eagerly await the landing of the next dart. Who is shooting and how they are doing it is not as important as where the dart lands. That is why taking a moment to appreciate the fortitude and heart of the physically limited player may not happen so often. And that is a most impressive part of the dart game.

There is such a broad range of prowess among darts enthusiasts that everyone can find a level at which they can compete. Participation in the effort to get the most from a person's innate ability through nurture and training is a shared experience. All participants recognize everyone is struggling with some degree of physical limitation, and the limitation is measured only by how close the dart lands to its intended target.

As many as 20 million people have darts as part of their life, just in America. Among these people are many who have extraordinary limitations but enjoy the added dimension to their life that darts offers. So I pause here to recognize the fortitude and heart of all those to whom we darts people may not ordinarily pay all that much attention. Here are the stories of four of them.

## Wayne

Wayne Crook is sixty-one years old and was introduced to darts while serving in the military during the early 1970s. The sport has intrigued, frustrated, excited, and challenged him for more than thirty-five years, even through difficulties.

A back injury made picking up darts from the floor difficult. His range of motion was limited to the point that picking up darts became embarrassing, and so he left league competition. A second uncorrectable back injury made picking darts up from the floor impossible, and his dart-playing days in public were over for a few years, but he continued to play at home. He figured out *how he could* instead of dwelling on *why he couldn't*.

On top of his existing difficulty, the driver of a crew cab truck going about 50 mph ran a stop sign and crashed into Wayne's vehicle. The result was the total destruction of Wayne's Blazer and, almost, him.

The most significant injuries were to his spine, which made it so, among other things, attempting to raise his head caused total loss of feeling and control to his right arm (he's right-handed).

It took three months of recovery and rehab before he could walk unassisted, and when he stood at the dartboard, he could only raise his head high enough to see the lower half of the board. All feeling and control of his right arm was lost. Fine motor skills like throwing darts and signing his name had to be relearned.

Regaining his dart game became his goal, and its improvement became the measure of his recovery. He was starting from scratch, and a darts learning program became his rehab program. His time was spent in wrist-finger thrust exercise, stroke development, and dart grouping practice. He began with two ten-minute sessions at the dartboard every day. In two months, his endurance improved, and he went to twenty-minute sessions. He became able to stick the darts within a circle of two inches or less. A month later, he could raise his head enough to see the entire dartboard, and he had regained feeling in his right arm. He has progressed to two sessions of twenty-five minutes, with one of them being a specific drill regimen designed to perfect accuracy.

*My goal is to achieve the accuracy and endurance I require to take on an open tournament. I believe this accident was simply an inconvenience that has provided the opportunity to make my game even better.*

## Jim

Jim Chatterton was sponsored for darts. Traveling to tournaments around the nation, he won the American Darts Organization ranking of fourteenth place. He suffered a brain stem stroke and remained hospitalized for several months. His whole world collapsed. His diagnosis for walking again was pretty slim, and he was also diagnosed with Gerstmann's syndrome. There are many factors involved with Gerstmann's syndrome, but the main ones are being unable to read or write, being unable to distinguish between the different fingers on the hand, permanent loss of sight on the affected side, and being unable to distinguish right from left.

The effects are permanent for Jim. He was wheelchair bound and entered intense therapy at a local neurological rehabilitation unit.

At home, alone and safe from embarrassment, he began throwing darts again. He slowly got used to his eyesight problems. His accuracy returned—albeit painfully slowly—and he had to relearn all the mathematical shots. He realized that all finishes are the result of patterns, and he still knew the patterns. Using this method, he was able to quickly reestablish all the mathematical shots back into his damaged brain.

It was a year later, after he got home, that he went out to play darts. His left side was still paralyzed; he was in a full-sized leg brace and had a hemi-walker to keep him stable. His left arm would not work, and he was unable to hold anything in his left hand. He had people pass his darts to him one at a time, and somebody else retrieved them from the board.

His arm gradually began to regain some strength, and he is now able to grip items like darts, knives, forks, etc., with little problem. He is unable to raise his arm very high, as his shoulder is constantly sore, but he is able to work around this problem. His eyesight never improved, and never will. He has sight through one-half of his right eye only. He is unable to read or write and has massive problems with anything remotely to do with mathematics. He has found methods and tricks to get around just about every problem he has. He has software in his laptop that reads and writes for him, and his cell phone has photographs of all his contacts.

He made his return to serious competition with appearances in four tournaments. Following the fourth tournament, he collapsed at the airport when he returned home. He was ill because he pushed his body too hard. He was very disappointed and did not play darts for over a month.

Two months later, he attended another tournament, and he came home determined to have one more go at darts aimed squarely at the top end, which is where he believes he belongs.

He began to practice again, with the Professional Darts Corporation's tournament in Chicago his goal. He joined an online darts learning program and received some valuable insight into what correct practice is all about and, more importantly, learned about the benefits of rest and recuperation. In short, he is listening to his body and being more professional in his approach to life in general, and in his approach to darts in particular.

*Darts is my main focus in life. It is the spur that is driving me to improve physically and mentally after my stroke. I am determined to get back amongst the top echelons of players, both here in the USA and back home in England (I am British, moving to the USA in 1999).*

## Glen

Glen R. Huff was born with cerebral palsy, and he walks with the aid of two canes.

He first got into darts while in college at Western Washington. They had a student recreational center with an assortment of pool and snooker tables, pinball machines, and one coiled paper dartboard on a corner wall of the room. He'd already tried his hand at the other recreations and decided to give darts a try since he was not good at pool, pinball, etc. He gave darts a try and liked it right from the start.

After graduating from WWU, he moved back home, discovered the local dart league, and got involved right away. He'd never had a sport growing up, and darts and the darts league were the first activities he found that gave him an "in," in that he could participate to the best of his ability and be accepted by his peers. His own particular stance setup and throw is different from the optimal style due to his legs being less stable than a non-handicapped person. He is short, at five feet tall, which has always made it harder for him to consistently get the darts to the top of the board.

He has over fifty books on darts in his darts library. Although he has a long way to go to get his own physical consistency and performance where he would like it to be, he is seeing improvements in his game from using what he found in one of his books. That improvement has brought a lot more enjoyment to the game for him.

He says he's been very fortunate in that he's made many wonderful friendships through the sport of darts—not only in his local league but also with folks halfway around the world, where the common love and appreciation of darts was enough to get a friendship started. Since 1987, he has traveled once a year to Las Vegas to watch the Las Vegas Desert Classic darts tournament; and as a pub league player, it's been a real thrill for him to see up close the professional dart players play. The chance to chat with them, and get photographs and autographs has been quite an experience over the years. One year at the Las Vegas Desert Classic, World Champions Phil Taylor and Bob Anderson gave him the darts they used, which was a real thrill for him. He is someone who collects dart sets, dartboards, books on the game, and tapes of darts matches. Getting such sets from the pros and getting to meet them has been something that he'll always treasure.

*I'll continue playing darts, whatever my level of ability, because it has given me so much over the years. One of the things that's kept me participating in darts for 25-plus years, is the fact that anyone can do it, men can play women, short players can play taller players, young players can play older players, and language differences are not a barrier, it's truly a great sport for all. I have always wished to get as many folks playing the game as possible; my thought being if I can play it, then anyone can play it.*

## Eileen

Eileen Willis started playing darts in 1976, still plays the game, and is captain of her dart team. She's had two incidents of injury during that time: an automobile accident and a fall at work. The automobile accident caused her seven months of recovery from face, breast, wrist, arm, and pelvis injury, but she didn't miss many of her dart team's matches through whole seven months. She sat on a stool and took her turn while others fetched her darts for her.

The fall has been another thing altogether. The damage to her lower back put her in a brace and caused her to use a cane. She took physical therapy, but not being able to walk or stand well eventually cost her, her job and put her on disability. Over time, she recovered enough that she can walk without the cane, but the injury has brought on arthritis in both hips and both knees. Prior to the accident, Eileen played darts seven days a week, but she has cut back severely after.

Since everyone has off days for one reason or another, her dart teammates see her as no different from everyone else. They care about her personally but see no other effect from her limitations. Each person shoots their darts as best as they can on each turn at the dartboard.

Eileen doesn't see her limitations having effect on her dart prowess. She believes she competes against the dartboard not the competitor and all limitations leave her mind while she is shooting her darts but when it comes to walking the 7'9" to retrieve the darts they come back.

She recalls being at the top rank of players as her high peak and intends to return to that level. She calls it going from peak to peak.

> *My darts go with me everywhere; weddings, funerals, baby showers, everywhere. And I don't care how old or decrepit I get I'll still be playing darts.*

# CONCLUSION

Now that the path I've to travel is shorter than the path I've traveled, I've had some time to consider the choices I've made, the influences which contributed to my making them, and the results of those choices.

Can't do anything about them—good or bad—but I can reflect upon the effects of them, and I can draw some conclusions and make some recommendations.

Select your vocation first by how much you enjoy it, and second by how much it pays.

Never deliberately set out to hurt someone.

Care for yourself so you can better care for those closest to you.

Share your sense of humor!

There are no manuals for life, our paths are determined by our experiences, opportunities and the choices we make.

CPSIA information can be obtained
at www.ICGtesting.com
Printed in the USA
LVOW04s2054120816
500060LV00016B/180/P

9 781682 072004